# *How*
# *to*
# *master*
# *networking*

Believe in
your dreams

Robyn H.

# DEDICATION

This book is dedicated to my nieces Kate and Greer—
networkers of the 21st century.

# How
# to
# master
# networking

## Robyn Henderson

**PRENTICE HALL**

Sydney   New York   Toronto   Mexico   New Delhi
London   Tokyo   Singapore   Rio de Janeiro

Aquisitions Editor: Kaylie Smith
Production Editor: Elizabeth Thomas
Copy Editor: Linda Morris
Cover design: Jack Jagtenberg
Typeset by James Young & Associates
Printed in Australia by Griffin Paperbacks, Adelaide

1 2 3 4 5 00 99 98 97

ISBN 0 7248 0527 3

**National Library of Australia
Cataloguing-in-Publication Data**

Henderson, Robyn.
    How to master networking.

    Includes index.
    ISBN 0 7248 0527 3

    1. Success in business. 2. Communication in management.
    3. Information networks. I. Title. (Series: Workwise series).

658.45

Prentice Hall of Australia Pty Ltd, *Sydney*
Prentice Hall, Inc., *Englewood Cliffs, New Jersey*
Prentice Hall Canada, Inc., *Toronto*
Prentice Hall Hispanoamericana, *SA, Mexico*
Prentice Hall of India Private Ltd, *New Delhi*
Prentice Hall International, Inc., *London*
Prentice Hall of Japan, Inc., *Tokyo*
Simon & Schuster (Asia) Pte Ltd, *Singapore*
Editora Prentice Hall do Brasil Ltda, *Rio de Janeiro*

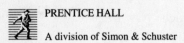

PRENTICE HALL

A division of Simon & Schuster

# *t*able *of* *c**o**n**t**e**n**t**s*

# *a*bout the author

Robyn Henderson is widely regarded as Australia's networking specialist, and as an international business educator she shows companies how to double their customer base through networking with integrity.

Robyn is the author and publisher of *Networking For $uccess* and *Are You The V.I.P. in Your Life?* as well as a self-mastery audiotape series. She is the co-founder of the East Coast Business Women's Network and was listed in the Top 100 Spirited Women of Australia (*New Woman* magazine, July 1994). She was also the winner of the 1995 Winning Woman Award from the Zonta Club of Hobart.

Robyn's career includes four years as a keynote speaker, 10 years in sales and telemarketing management and, prior to this, 13 years in the hospitality industry. She has clear insight into prospecting and networking—the business building skills of the 1990s. Robyn openly shares simple strategies and skills to enable you and your company to achieve your full potential *now*. Robyn is a speaker who 'walks her talk'—she gets results. If your business needs a kick start, start networking with Robyn Henderson today!

# *t*he *WorkWise* series

The *WorkWise* series will provide readers with the skills and techniques to improve personal and business productivity. Based on sound management principles, all the books in the series are written in a practical and easy-to-read style.

To enhance their easy-to-use format, the books are filled with practical ideas and illustrative examples which reinforce concepts and provide a handy and reliable resource for anyone interested in boosting their personal and business success.

The books in the *WorkWise* series will help anyone who is in the workforce, or looking to join the workforce, who is keen to improve their work skills with a view to enhancing their productivity and accomplishments.

Forthcoming topics in the series include:

> time management
> resume writing
> telephone techniques
> conducting meetings
> self-motivation
> supervision
> performance appraisal
> negotiation
> writing a marketing plan
> personal investment
> working from home.

The *WorkWise* series is a joint publishing venture between the Australian Institute of Management (AIM) Training Centre and Prentice Hall Australia Pty Limited. Enquiries about books in the series, or information regarding the submission of manuscripts, should be directed to either AIM or Prentice Hall.

# *i*ntroduction

In today's competitive marketplace it is critical that we understand one simple philosophy—people want to do business with people they know and trust, or with someone who knows someone they know and trust.

One of the quickest ways we can grow our own business is to assist others to grow theirs. True networkers believe there is plenty for everyone—plenty of clients, plenty of new customers, plenty of great ideas, plenty of opportunities. At this point in time they may not be in your own network but one day they may be. However, there are only two sorts of people in the world: those you know and those you don't know yet. Some of the people you know could put you in touch with those you don't know.

This book has been written in such a way that you do not have to read it from cover to cover. You may select a chapter on a networking sector that interests you and read about it. It has also been written in a workbook format to enable you to apply these networking principles to your own business.

Throughout the book we will be showing you ways to:

❍ earn the right to do business;

❍ generate endless referrals;

❍ give without 'hooks'; and

❍ avoid losing customers.

## KEY POINT

*In the networking environment it is not who you know, but who knows you.*

# *n* etworking quiz

Take a few moments to answer the following questions and gauge just where you rate on our networking meter.

Please circle your preferred response.

1. In the last seven days, have you exchanged business cards with every stranger you have met and spoken to for more than one minute, both in and out of work?                    Yes    No

2. Have you given a referral to someone in your network in the last seven days?                    Yes    No

3. Are you currently a financial member of at least two networks—for example, associations, chambers of commerce, sporting or cultural groups, business networks?                    Yes    No

4. Do you attend a networking group at least once a week?                    Yes    No

5. Have you sent one or more cards (thank you, birthday, congratulations etc.) this week?                    Yes    No

6. Does your current business card state your name, what business you are in, what you specialise in and your contact details on it clearly?                    Yes    No

7. Does every staff member in your company have a business card?                    Yes    No

8. Are you still doing business with every customer who has ever done business with your company since its inception?                    Yes    No

9. Are you regularly helping other associates grow their business as well as growing your own?                    Yes    No

10. Do you have a system in place where you record your wins or accomplishments daily?                    Yes    No

continued ...

## Scoring

Score 1 point for every Yes answer and 0 points for every No answer.

| | |
|---|---|
| If you scored **9–10 out of 10** | Congratulations! You are a great networker. Reading this book will give you a competitive edge on networking towards the year 2000. |
| If you scored **5–8 out of 10** | Well done. Make reading this book a priority for you over the next week. With little effort, you can really grow your business/career. Make this your best year yet. |
| If you scored **0–4 out of 10** | Start reading now. Take the morning off, relax. The networking world may have confused you previously. After reading this book you will be able to create unlimited opportunities to enhance your business and personal network. |

# 1

# *What is networking?*

The key to networking in the 1990s is:

*earning the right to ask a favour—giving without hooks.*

Throughout this chapter I will discuss why networking has become the number one business building tool throughout the 1990s. Many professions are almost totally referral-based—for example, the legal profession, accountants, life insurance agents, real estate agents and many sales areas. Think about the last referral you gave someone. Had the person earned the right to receive that referral? More than likely the person had already done something for you, either in a professional sense by doing a great job, or in a personal sense by doing you a favour.

If your business is referral-generated and you find that your supply of referrals has dried up, you may have taken referrals for granted—a number one no-no in the networking world.

Generally there are two ways to grow a business:

1. gain new customers;

2. encourage current customers to buy more products more often.

## Earning the right to do business

Networking plays a part in both of these areas. Networking can generate referrals for you and attract new business. At the same time networking with your current customers can enthuse them to buy more often and try additional products or services. Either way we earn the right to ask a favour or earn the right to ask for business.

'Giving without hooks' is a concept that many people have a difficulty accepting. For example, when attending a dinner or a social event we may meet someone for the first time and they share with us that they are renovating their home. They describe in great detail a problem they are having and 'without hooks' you explain to them how you had overcome that same situation yourself; possibly the material you used, how you went about it, whatever it took you to fix the problem.

Once you had shared the information, you did not pull out an invoice book and charge them. You just gave the information away—without hooks. You did not expect anything in return. In fact it was a win situation. Your new acquaintance appreciated the information that you were happy to share with them. From now on you will be remembered positively by that person.

As another example, you may be shopping for a car. You visit a variety of car yards that are selling cars both within your budget and a little beyond it. You may find an extremely helpful car salesperson who goes to no end of trouble to assist with your purchase. Unfortunately, the cars on offer are far beyond your budget. You thank the dealer for being so helpful and, although you don't buy a car there, that helpful dealer stays in your mind.

When the occasion arises and you are asked for a referral to a car dealer, that person comes to mind. If you have kept their business card (assuming you were given one in the first place) you will more than likely refer that dealer to the person wanting to buy from that range of cars.

Yes, the car dealer was probably disappointed when they did not make a sale with you. However, being a great networker, they realise they may have missed out this time but they have left a positive impression for the next time that their range of cars is mentioned.

Great networkers look at the big picture. Sometimes networking brings business overnight. Other times referrals come from encounters from weeks or months previously.

To enable you to gain from reading this book, we have included worksheets so that you can really gauge where your business is heading, how good a networker you are and what areas you can improve on. You will gain more from this book if you write your answers as you go. It will also serve as a great reminder of your progress as a networker.

## *KEY POINTS*

*In the networking environment, it is not who you know, rather who knows you.*

*The basic key to networking is to earn the right to do business and earn the right to ask a favour.*

| | | |
|---|---|---|
| When was the last time someone asked you for a favour? _____ | | |
| Did you willingly oblige? (circle your response) | Yes | No |
| If not, why not? _____ | | |
| If yes, did that person genuinely thank you for your assistance? | Yes | No |
| What form did their thank you take? | Written? | Verbal? |
| More importantly, will you provide assistance for that person in the future? | Yes | No |
| Reverse the situation: when was the last time you asked someone for a favour? _____ | | |
| Did they willingly oblige? | Yes | No |
| If yes, had you previously earned the right to ask a favour? | Yes | No |
| If so, how? _____ | | |
| If not, why do you think that person said no? _____ | | |
| How did you say thank you to this person? | Verbal? | Written? |
| Will you feel comfortable asking this person for assistance in the future? | Yes | No |

Regardless of how you responded above, this person is now part of your network. If they have earned the right to ask a favour, generally we are happy to help them. If they have not earned that right, or if they did not show appreciation the last time we helped them, we may be reluctant to offer assistance this time.

# 2

# *Every best friend was once a perfect stranger*

## How to turn suspects into advocates via networking

This chapter will discuss the importance of building relationships with people, including those new to our network as well as already firmly established contacts. Many people make the mistake of meeting people and assuming that they will automatically want to buy their product or service, just because you have met them. Wrong!

Every day many people are missing chances to do business, largely because they don't take the time to build a relationship with a person or even bother to get to know them.

Figure 2.1  The Customer Ladder of Loyalty

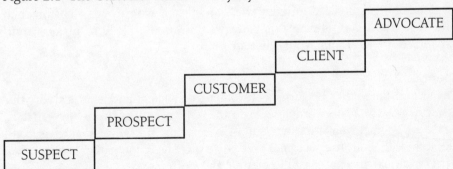

## The customer ladder of loyalty

Many companies make the mistake of building their businesses on lots of customers and very few clients. Many of us are already familiar with the customer ladder of loyalty (see Figure 2.1). We see the ladder rising from:

Suspect—Prospect—Customer—Client—Advocate

### Suspects

In the real estate areas suspects may be defined as:

○ anyone over, say, 21 years of age living in or wanting to invest in a certain area and who are financially eligible to buy or sell a property.

### Prospects

These people become prospects when they:

○ make the decision to purchase a property;

○ start reading the real estate newspaper advertisements;

○ start visiting real estate offices;

○ start asking friends and associates questions such as: Who did you buy your home from? Were you happy with the service you received? Was there any after-sales service? Would you go back to that real estate agent again? (The last question is really the most critical. If they would not go back to that agent, all the great service that agent gave, or thought they gave, is totally wasted. The customer will not bother to refer business back to them.)

### Customer

Again, using the real estate scenario, the day a person buys or sells a property they become a customer. In a banking scenario, a customer may open one account with that bank. A person may have a haircut at a new salon. The critical key to business growth is turning that customer into a client—encouraging that person to make a second-time purchase. In the book *The Power of One on One* by Ian Kennedy and Bryce Courtenay, we learn that if we can get a customer to make a second-time purchase, they are 10 times more likely to make a third and, ultimately, to become your advocate.

### Client

This second-time purchase turns a customer into a client and is critical for your business growth. Many companies use the 'churn and burn' policy—that is, attract a customer, make a quick sale, never follow up, never make a second sale, forget all about the customer and move on. These companies rarely attract clients and rarely reach their full potential as a business.

*How to master networking*

Some companies would believe that their business is different and people only need their services once. That may be true in some cases, however this is where the power of referral is vital. If a customer was happy with the one-off service/product provided by a business, they will refer more business to you. This is the critical loop that connects the customer with the client and ultimately with the advocate.

**Advocates**

List the names of five advocates in your current network:

1. _____

2. _____

3. _____

4. _____

5. _____

Was there anything that you did out of the ordinary to turn these customers into advocates? If so, list them below.

1. _____

2. _____

3. _____

4. _____

5. _____

Do you only make contact with these advocates when you want something from them—for example, a referral? (circle your response)    Yes          No

Would you have made contact with these advocates in the last 90 days?    Yes          No

How often do you let these advocates know how much you value their business as well as their referrals? _____

What systems do you have in place to give these advocates recognition on a regular basis? _____

What systems could be introduced to give your advocates recognition

(a) monthly?

*continued …*

*Every best friend was once a perfect stranger*

(b) quarterly?

(c) annually?

What dollar value would you place on the referral business that each of these advocates gives freely to you each year?

1. _____

2. _____

3. _____

4. _____

5. _____

Total: $

## Customers

How many customers do you currently have (approximately)? _____

What percentage of your customer base are clients (i.e. second-time purchasers)?

_____

What percentage of your customer base are advocates? _____

How long has your business been operating? _____

Since inception, how many customers have you had? _____

What are some of the reasons why customers have stopped buying from you?

_____

_____

Finally, estimate the approximate dollar value of your annual turnover assuming that you had never lost a customer. _____

If this is your current turnover, congratulations. If not, read on to find out how to turn customers into advocates.

How big would your business be if you never lost a customer? The obvious answer is: probably much bigger than it is now. For example, suppose your product or service is worth $100 per sale.

○ What would next month's sales be worth to your company if everyone who had ever used your product or service bought something from you next month?

○ What are you expecting next month's sales to be?

There is normally a large difference between the answers to the above questions. Throughout the book we will be addressing this issue. If we can stop losing our customers and start valuing them and their networks, then our businesses will be much healthier.

Let's look at ways to nurture our network and give recognition to our clients. Take a moment to answer the following questions.

Throughout this book, I will show you simple systems to help you:

○ give regular recognition to your customers, clients and advocates;

○ show value to your current network; and

○ generate and keep new business.

You are invited to open your mind to new ideas and unlimited opportunities in the exciting world of networking.

### KEY POINTS
*The definition of networking is to earn the right to ask a favour.*

*If you never lose a customer, your business will grow steadily based on the volume of referrals you receive from people who have already done business with you.*

# 3

# *Business cards—your most important networking tool*

This chapter will explain why business cards are absolutely critical for effective networking in today's busy world. Without a business card you cannot do business. Start turning your business cards into business today.

In our busy lives we meet so many people both in our business and personal life. It is so easy to forget names and faces. For very busy people, everyone starts to look the same at times. We sit with someone at a networking function and we are sure we have met them somewhere before, we just don't know where. Business cards help us to identify people, remember who they are and know what it is that they do.

How many business cards would you give out if you knew that every business card would turn into a referral, a new customer or repeat business? Hundreds? Thousands? More than likely a lot more business cards than you are currently giving out. Your business card is your silent salesperson. For this one reason, it is absolutely critical that your card reflects exactly what you do.

Your business card must include:

O your name

O your phone number (including STD code)

O your occupation.

Sounds obvious, doesn't it. However, look at the pile of business cards you have collected recently. Can you remember who does what? John Smith & Associates could be a law firm, plumbers, electricians, architects—who would know? Many companies make the mistake of assuming everyone knows what they do. This can sometimes be quite a foolish and costly assumption. Someone new to the city, or the country for that matter, may not know one firm from another. Some large corporations also miss out on business by assuming their name is sufficient information for recognition. People may have heard of your company but they may not realise all the areas that you cover. If a business card only states the company name and the company has a 10 storey building housing the main office, some potential clients may think: they are too big, they would not want a small business like me. This may not be entirely accurate.

If a business card states the company's speciality areas on its reverse side, this often takes the guess work out of new business.

Are you making it hard for people to do business with you?

Does your business card clearly state:

O what you do?

O what your specialty area is?

O your phone, fax, mobile and pager numbers?

O where your other branches and offices are located?

O when you are open for business (if this is out of normal business hours)?

## Does your business card need a revamp?

*Dynamic Small Business* magazine commissioned a survey of 600 business cards in 1993. This survey revealed that:

○ 42 per cent of the business cards did not state the nature of the business and one in every six cards gave no other clues;

○ 20 per cent did not include any name and 2 per cent had no surname;

○ 49 per cent had no title, among them a significant number of people working for government departments;

○ 32 per cent did not include an STD code;

○ 5 per cent gave no address;

○ 3 per cent printed the address on the back;

○ 34 per cent did not include their State;

○ 3 per cent had no postcode.

*Source:* Copyright © *Dynamic Small Business*, August–September 1993. Reproduced with permission of the editor.

### Suggestions

○ Use the back of your business card to list things such as additional services, speciality areas, your mission statement or your company motto.

○ If you are in a competitive area, you may consider including a photo on the front of your card. This will make it much easier for people to remember you.

   *Important tip*: make sure you have your photo taken by a professional photographer. Cutting costs on do-it-yourself shots or taking a snap from your wedding album may save you dollars in the short term. However, this may cost you business in the long term. If you want to be treated as a professional, you must create a professional image. You only have one chance to make a first impression.

○ Highlight the main phone number in bold.

○ Bilingual cards are a must if you are planning to do business in non-English speaking countries. The art of handing out business cards is a time-honoured tradition in the Chinese community. They are giving you a summary of themselves in the form of a business card. You are expected to acknowledge the card, comment on the content and treat the card with respect. Working with the Australian Chinese Chamber of Commerce in Perth, I learned that the Chinese invented networking and the Japanese perfected it. A Japanese business person will give you a business card every time you meet, whether you have met them before or not. Australians normally only exchange business cards at the initial meeting. The Japanese belief is that the more cards you have, the more business you can refer to others. Again, this makes it very easy to refer business to others.

○ Multiple business cards are a must if you have a number of businesses that are non-related. An example of false economy is having one business card to state that you are an image consultant, fashion designer, tarot reader etc. Don't laugh, there are many business cards in the marketplace that are doing more damage than benefit.

If you have a number of areas to your business, use two or more cards as required. Decide before you go to a function what 'hat' you will be wearing and make sure you have sufficient cards in stock. Only give a second card to someone if you feel the 'other' business is more appropriate.

○ If you are linked up to the Internet, be sure to include your Internet address in bold on your business card. Again, make it easy for people to do business with you. As we move into the 21st century, E-mail and Internet addresses will become standard communication for all businesses. E-mail is a fabulous time saver as you can send or respond to messages in a fraction of the time that it would take to write and send a fax or make a phone call. E-mail response pages are pretyped so that you need only enter your response and, with the push of a button, send your message. The Internet is really a global network of millions of computer users. Savvy Internet users offer an E-mail response form on their home page to assist with generating instant responses to interested users.

○ Colour business cards are becoming very popular. Originally, I had a black and white photo on my business card which I have since converted to an attractive colour business card. People appear to place a greater value on a colour card and are reluctant to throw away a card with your photo on it. My printer assures me once you have a colour card, you will never go back to a standard card. After collecting business cards at one of my networking presentations, I am always pleased when there are a number of photo business cards, as it helps to jog my memory on the interaction I may have had with that person.

○ People may find it beneficial to have two kinds of business cards and, depending on where they are and the image they want to portray, they may use the more conservative card or the more colourful. I recently met a 'tax slasher' who introduced me to a 'profit builder'. When I asked them more about their work, I made the comment, you sound like you do similar work to an accountant. They replied that they were in fact accountants but if they had told me that initially, they would never have had the opportunity to describe to me in detail what they did. Hats off to the 'tax slasher'.

○ Vertical and horizontal cards are available. From experience, I have found that a standard size card is important. If you have a lot of information to include, you may choose a card that will fold down to a standard size. Alternatively, you may choose a bookmark-size card that also folds down to a standard size. I have observed people discarding cards that are odd shapes and sizes because they are too difficult to store.

○ A good business card will fit into a standard business card holder. It will therefore be 90 mm x 50 mm in size and be printed on card that weighs approximately 280 gsm (grams per square metre).

○ It is important to develop a good relationship with your printer. Shop around until you find one who understands your needs. When you see an eye-catching business card, ask the owner which printer they use—word of mouth is the best referral. Be upfront in explaining your budgetary restrictions (if you have any). Good printers know that your printing needs will increase in direct relation to the growth of your business. A small account today, when nurtured, will grow into a large account. I encourage a

---

**HOT TIP**

If the thought of giving out a business card terrifies you, try role playing with friends or staff members. I prefer to give my card out when I introduce myself to people, in the following way:

'Hi, I'm Robyn Henderson, what's your name?'

They can then see what it is that you do and that's it. You don't have to talk about you and can begin by talking about them. I always steer the conversation away from me and place the emphasis on the other person. If they are good networkers, they will automatically give you their card, or they may mention they don't have a card with them. Never make anyone feel uncomfortable for not having a card (you might like to offer them a spare blank card that you have in order for them to write down their details—refer to this section in Chapter 4).

Practising in front of a mirror also works well. If you are new to business card giving, I guarantee you it will only be during the first four or five 'givings' that you will feel self-conscious. After that it will become very natural for you. Anyone will talk to you for 15 minutes if you are not speaking about yourself.

---

wide use of cards, stationery etc. If you don't get good service from a printer, tell them. If you do get good service, tell others.

○ When exchanging business cards, always put the cards you receive in one place—for example, if your own business cards are in your left pocket, place the cards you are receiving in your right pocket in order to avoid confusion when giving out your own card. If you are using a business card holder, have your business cards in the front and put other people's business cards at the back.

Let me share with you a real success story from a member of an audience I spoke to in Canberra. As you will learn, I encourage people to attend one networking function per week and give out 50 business cards each week. I met up with a banking business development manager a couple of months after she first attended one of my presentations. Her name was Allison. She had taken my suggestions on board and started attending functions and exchanging business cards, although initially she was quite nervous. She met a business woman at a function, exchanged a card and then thought to herself, Robyn told us to follow up and send something to the person we met. In a dilemma as to what might interest this woman, she forwarded a copy of the bank's annual report with a handwritten note. The women rang to thank her for her effort and made the comment that even her own bank did not go to this much trouble.

One month later the woman rang Allison to ask her if she could transfer 'some investments' that were maturing. The amount—$1 million! That's networking!

**KEY POINT**
*Turn your business cards into business.*

AUSTRALIA'S NETWORKING
SPECIALIST

Robyn Henderson

P.O. Box 195, Coogee, N.S.W. 2034,
Australia
Tel: (02) 369 1025   Fax: (02) 369 1053

# 4

# *Building a networking relationship*

This chapter will explain what to do with all the business cards you exchange and how to turn business cards into referrals and unlimited networking opportunities.

## What will you do with the business cards you collect?

Many people I know have great stacks of business cards in their top drawers with rubber bands holding them together. Every year they go through these cards, realise they don't know one person from another and throw them all out. Your goal as a successful networker is to exchange 50 business cards every week and have a system in place to manage these exchanged cards.

Giving out a business card is step one. Exchanging cards with the people that we meet is the target of all successful networkers. If you are not used to giving out business cards, one of the key things to do is to make sure your cards are always easily accessible. You may choose to carry them in your jacket pocket or in a business card holder.

Cards must be readily available for use to take full advantage of networking opportunities. Women often change handbags or briefcases to attend an event. Make sure you have a supply of business cards in each of your handbags, your briefcase, your wallet and your car.

Occasionally you may find people reluctant to give you their business card. I have found some people really size you up as to whether you are 'worth' receiving one of their cards. As they reluctantly hand it to me, I usually say, 'You don't have to give me a card, I was just hoping to refer business to you at some stage in the future. That's how I've built my business in the last four years, by helping others to grow theirs.' This generally throws them. Seriously though, don't be offended if they don't want to give you a card—it is really their loss.

## Blank cards

Many people do not have business cards or forget to carry cards with them when they attend networking functions. A simple solution is for you to carry a number of blank business cards (available at most stationers in packs of 50). Once you have built up a rapport with someone, you may choose to offer them a blank card on which to write their details so you can keep in touch with them.

Some people choose to use their own cards to write someone else's details on them. This is really just a waste of your cards. Always carry blank cards in addition to your own cards. You will be surprised how often you get to use them.

Many companies only supply business cards to the senior and middle management. There is no faster way to build self-esteem in a staff member and help to build their loyalty to the company than by giving them a business card and encouraging them to give out cards to all their friends and relatives.

If the average person over 25 years of age knows at least 1000 people, would it be fair to say that some of those people may be in the need of your product or service? How can they do business with you if they don't know how to contact you? Value the resources you have within your own organisations; your staff are your greatest investment. Encourage them to network also.

| | | |
|---|---|---|
| How many business cards do you have in stock today? _____ | | |
| If you plan to give out 50 business cards per week, will you need to order more cards this week? (circle your response) | Yes | No |
| Based on what you have already read, do you think you need to revamp your business card? If so, how and when will you revamp it? _____ | Yes | No |
| Do all your staff/co-workers have business cards? | Yes | No |

Include a business card with every piece of correspondence you send by mail. People will often throw away your letter but they will keep your card.

Let's assume that after reading this book, you start to give out business cards to every person that you meet and, ideally, receive a card in return. You will soon end up with quite a collection of cards. Read on for some valuable tips on what to do with these cards so they don't end up in huge meaningless bundles.

Taking 10 minutes out of your busy schedule to action your business cards is critical. You will often have paid to attend a function, spent one or more hours of your time attending and made valuable connections. *Following up within 72 hours is critical.*

## What will I do with all these business cards?

Some people underestimate their memory's potential. By writing a few notes on the back of the card, it gives us memory joggers—the date and place are critical information. Write down something you remember about the person. In Chapter 5, we will be talking about the power of recognition in detail. Good networkers are able to generate conversations with people that are not work based. Finding out what someone does for fun, how they spend their weekends, what their interests are—these are the types of things you would write when listing something to remember about the person.

Figure 4.1  What will I do with all these business cards?

On the back of every business card
you receive, write:

- the date you met the person

- where you met them

- any action required

FILE

Can you imagine someone ringing you today, who was able to quote the topic of conversation they had with you four months ago when you first met? Would you be impressed? I certainly would.

## Wowing customers

In the last four years I have presented the keys to successful networking to thousands of people. My observation throughout Australia and New Zealand is that approximately 80 per cent of the population does not get recognition on the job. They work for managers who constantly catch them doing something wrong and rarely catch them doing something right. That means that around 80 per cent of your customers don't receive recognition in their lives either. Recognition is the single thing that you can give them with a minimum of effort and expense on your part.

This simple fact is the reason why networking is so powerful. We give people recognition, we give them something that is missing in their life and something most people crave for. When you give recognition to someone, you WOW them. Think about the last time someone sent you a thank you note, an unexpected card, a magazine article—anything that showed you that they were thinking about you in a non-work related way. Were you impressed? Of course you were. It takes so little to show people that you care and, as the old saying goes, people don't care how much you know until they know how much you care.

Successful networkers wow a customer every day (see Chapter 5). First, we have to establish what will wow them. The only way we find that out is to ask them questions about themselves, about their interests and then listen to their response. Giving someone 60 seconds of uninterrupted time and undivided eye contact is far better than 10 minutes of only half listening, with your eyes darting around the room. The brief notes you make on a person's card can act as a trigger to wow this person.

## Is any action required?

Most salespeople lose sales because they don't follow up. Are you guilty of this? Check your in-tray. Are you embarrassed to get back to some of these people because it has been so long? Remember the key to networking—we *earn* the right to get business. That right often comes from getting back to people more than once to answer their queries. If you have met someone at a networking function or a social event, honour your commitment and follow up.

At times my systems let me down and I find a business card with a note on the back and realise I have not actioned it, or I find correspondence that is long overdue. My advice for this situation is to be honest—they are human too. For example, 'Apologies for taking so long to get back to you. Your card was buried in my in-tray—hope I am not too late to give you this information.' This is far better than never getting back to them and then being embarrassed the next time you see them.

A handwritten note (approximately 25 words) is sometimes the most powerful networking tool. Everyone is busy, no one has time to waste. A personal note attached to your brochure or proposal can enhance the lasting impression you leave with your contact. For example:

> Hi Mary, great to meet you at Sue and Keith's wedding. You mentioned you may be interested in purchasing a mobile phone. Have enclosed the latest brochure on our top of the range digitals. Call me if I can answer any queries.
> Regards,
>
> Robyn.
>
> PS Hope your daughter's birthday party was a great success on Sunday.

This brief note may take one minute to write and cost you maybe one dollar in stationery (including postage). What impact will this have on Mary when she receives it? Many people make the mistake of thinking that if we meet people in a social environment, it is not business and we don't have to follow up or, even worse, it's not appropriate to follow up. Wrong on both counts. Non-work related events are more and more becoming the environment where business is being done in the marketplace.

| | | |
|---|---|---|
| Is there anyone you have met in the last fortnight who is still waiting to be followed up? (circle your response) | Yes | No |
| What action can you take today to reconnect with this person? _____ | | |
| Have you missed opportunities in the past because you did not follow up? | Yes | No |
| Is it possible to rectify that now? | Yes | No |

It is not appropriate to phone and just ask for the business. However, you may consider making a call, reconnecting with the person and aiming to rebuild the rapport that you had when you first met. It's a bit like building a bridge. You are one of the foundations and they are on the other side of the river as the other foundation. The more contact you make with them, the more the bridge comes together. Trust is the cement or pins that keeps the bridge standing until it finally joins in the middle.

So now there is someone in our network with mutual trust and respect. This does not happen overnight—we develop trust and earn respect. Remember, we have not earned the right to ask the favour—yet.

### KEY POINT
*Always follow up an exchange of business cards promptly. Have your networking stationery ready for action.*

# Time management for effective networking

This chapter will explain how to make time for networking and how important this time management is for your business growth.

If tonight at midnight, a group of people were given 24 gold bars and told to invest them wisely and return the following night at midnight, the returning group would include:

○ people who now had more than 24 gold bars;

○ people who had less than 24 gold bars; and

○ people who had squandered the entire 24 gold bars.

The combinations are endless. Every day we are given 24 hours—no more, no less. The first person to come up with a way people can buy time without having to change any of their current habits will be a millionaire many times over. Each day we have:

$$24 \text{ hours} = 1440 \text{ minutes} = 86\,440 \text{ seconds}$$

In my opinion the world's leading time-management guru is Stephen Covey, author of *Seven Habits of Highly Effective People*, and *First Things First*. Both of these books are highly recommended to sharpen your time-management skills.

## Income building versus income generating

So, where do we find time to network?

Our business time is largely split between:

○ income building; and

○ income generating.

Income generating for most of us is going to work and producing whatever it is we produce to earn our income. Income building is something we do to lay the foundations for future income generation. Networking is part of income building.

Take real estate agents as an example. They buy and sell properties for people. Selling the properties generates the income. Networking generates the listings to give them the properties that will generate the income. If they don't have any listings, they have probably not been networking effectively. Networking for real estate agents may include:

○ valuing and making contact with their past buyers and vendors on a regular basis;

○ giving the above group referrals on a regular basis;

○ regularly attending networking functions (chambers of commerce, community groups, sporting functions) in their area;

○ introducing themselves to new businesses in their area;

○ making contact after the sale has gone through—that is, after-sales service.

Every business must look at how it is actively attracting new business as well as valuing current customers. As our advertising dollar becomes more costly, for every $100 spent, a portion of that budget needs to be spent in two areas:

1. attracting new clients

2. valuing old customers

---

What networking activities do you do for your business?

Does networking have a top priority in your     Yes          No
business? (circle your response)

If not, why not? _____

Effective networkers have systems in place to save time with their networking. If they are allocating a minimum of 30 minutes a day to network (this excludes attending any networking functions) then it is important that they have all their networking needs to hand. These may include:

O *Stationery:* Thank you notes, congratulations cards, sympathy cards, birthday cards, get well cards etc. (The more prompt your response the more powerful your impact.)

O *Promotional material about your company or business:* Refer to Chapter 2— send a follow up within 72 hours of meeting the person requesting information.

O *Stamps:* Again, a prompt response impresses people.

O *Address books/directory for referring contacts within your networks:* This may be a manual system—a small business card holder/book style with, say, cards from your top 10 clients. You will be able to give their business cards out as the opportunity arrives to promote their business. Make sure you have written on the back of their card 'referred by (insert your name)'. This way they will track that referral back to you. (More details on this will be provided in Chapter14—Revenue enhancement.)

## KISS—Keep It Simple Stupid

Again, a well known saying—the simpler the systems, the more we will action them.

The above suggestions may sound obvious, however, as those gold bars of time slide through your fingers, it is really easy to put networking tasks off because they don't seem that urgent.

### KEY POINT
*Networking is a number one priority every day if you want
your business to grow.*

The more you network actively, the more networking becomes part of your life and you will include it as a top priority for your day. However, for novice networkers, 30 minutes per day is a *must*. Ideally a 60-minute daily networking time slot will gain fast results for you. Within this 30 or 60 minute time frame, decide how much time to allocate to:

O current/past clients; and

O new/potential clients.

We need to look at both areas, not just new business. We want to develop a habit of making contact with past clients regularly—not just when we want new business from them. We should aim to contact them three to four times per year, over and above the times when we are supplying our product or service. This may vary slightly for some professions—for example, in real estate, an agent who has not contacted a previous vendor or buyer for three or more years may be horrified at the prospect of making contact four times this year. If we include, for example:

○ a Christmas card;

○ a 'saw this and thought of you' newspaper or magazine clipping; and

○ two company newsletters or chat sheets,

then our four contacts a year are quite achievable. Once we have the customer's details on our database, it is simply a matter of deciding how often we want to make contact and doing it. Some businesses make the mistake of only networking when they have no orders in the in-tray at all. This is too late, you will receive some business straight away, other business will take time to develop. If you are continually networking, you never run out of work. Other businesses, such as hairdressing salons may be seeing their client every 4–7 weeks, depending on the client's needs—for exampe, cut, colour, perm etc. What systems would a hairdresser need to have in place just to notice if a client did not come in for their regular visit? I have visited many hairdressers over my 40 plus years, and to this day have never had a phone call or note saying: 'Just a reminder that it's four weeks since your last cut, should we hold a slot for you in the next two weeks? You normally see us on Saturday mornings.' My firm belief is that business is there for the taking, and not to be stolen from your competitors. It is simply a matter of keeping in touch, and keeping your name and your business name in front of the customer's face regularly.

## Daily networking plan

Successful networkers are organised. Thirty minutes a day spent on networking is a valuable investment of time. You can't spare 30 minutes a day? Ask yourself:

○ What am I doing that doesn't really have to be done?

○ What am I doing that could be done by someone else?

○ What can I delegate today?

○ What am I doing that could be done more efficiently?

O What am I doing that wastes the time of others?

O What is my biggest time waster?

O What can I do today to reduce this time wasting?

When you are looking at the effectiveness of your time management and wondering where you are going to find that additional 30–60 minutes per day for networking, get a second opinion on the questions listed above. You may like to ask some of your fellow workers to answer those questions on your behalf. Often they see things quite differently to you.

The only difference between your normal 'to do' list and the planning sheet shown in Figure 5.2 is the inclusion of time allocation. Most of us write 'to do' lists for a 36-hour day and then beat ourselves up when we don't get through everything in our 24-hour day. Hopefully, the time management sheet will allow you to schedule time for networking. Be it a 15 or 30-minute time slot, it is imperative you know what you will be doing in that time.

You may choose to adapt this sheet in your diary and use it as your weekly networking plan or as a daily sheet. Either way, whatever does not get done today, you can do tomorrow.

Remember to focus your networking time—50 per cent of the time on old customers and 50 per cent on new business. We need to keep both sides in perspective to grow our business to its full potential. Some progressive companies today also use this principle with their advertising dollar—50 per cent showing their current customers how much they value them and 50 per cent looking for new business. Unfortunately, companies and professions only focussing on new business and not valuing their current and past businesses will ultimately end up out of business.

### KEY POINT
*Remember your current customers—make some form of contact every 90 days—other than sending an account.*

Time management tips for your 15 to 60-minute networking time.

1. Allocate uninterrupted time. (If you were with a VIP client this would happen.) Networking must take a high priority because you are the most important person in your life. If you aren't, why not?

2. Utilise your 'on hold' time on the phone, arrive early for appointments and spend a few extra moments in the car to write a few notes. Stolen minutes here and there add up to hours. The more recognition you give to your customers, the more your business will grow (see Chapter 9).

Figure 5.1 Daily Planning

Date:                                    Day:

## DAILY  PLANNING SHEET

Today's priority jobs:              Time allocated:

1. _____

2. _____

3. _____

4. _____

5. _____


Today's phone calls:




Tomorrow's calls & projects:

3. Allocate a set day for writing birthday cards for that month. Place a small pencil mark on the envelope indicating the day the card has to be mailed to arrive on time (see Chapter 9).

4. Have your Christmas cards printed earlier in the year. Start writing personal messages on the cards rather than just your company name. It's the little things that count. That personalised reference to a golf handicap, planned Christmas holiday or house renovation will make your card stand out from the dozens of impersonal cards landing on the desk.

5. Carry thank you notes in your diary or briefcase. After leaving a client's office, take a moment to write a short 'thank you for your time' note and drop it in the mail on the way back to your office.

6. Make your job easier by employing effective networkers—head hunters are well aware how important networking skills are to a company's growth. There are only two sorts of people in the world—those you know and those you don't know yet. Some of your staff may already know the people you are wanting to meet. Ask them.

7. Start to take note of things that impress you with service and customer satisfaction. When you experience great service, write a note to the company and, of course, include your business card.

8. Include your business card with every item you send by mail—your credit card bills, electricity, orders, thank you cards etc. Remember, your business cards are your silent salespeople. Make sure your cards are working for you.

9. Buy stationery in bulk. Having cards on hand is critical. If you have to go out and buy a thank you card everytime you need one, you will never do it. Most printers are happy to provide a personalised range of stationery to suit all your networking needs.

10. Read daily newspapers and send letters of congratulations to people who achieve things you admire, whether you know them or not. Business is often done with people new to a position or location (sporting or political transfer) purely because you take the time to acknowledge their achievement.

11. Send a thank you card when you *don't* get the business. I repeat, send a thank you card when you don't get the business—you will certainly stand out from your competitors. Okay, so you did not get the business now, but maybe the successful provider fails to deliver. Who will more than likely get second choice? The one who stands out from the crowd for doing exceptional things.

Back in 1993, I trained long-term unemployed students in telemarketing. I encouraged them to go for job interviews and you can imagine the psyching up that occurred prior to their interviews. Sometimes they missed out and their self-esteem would plummet. I encouraged them (at times, forced them) to send a 'thank you for advising me I did not get the job' letter. One hundred people may have applied for the job, 10 received interviews, one got the job, more than likely only one sent a 'thank you for not giving me the job'. Would you consider this person if the first person did not work out, or you found you needed more staff?

Networkers are persistent. They only have 24 hours in a day, so they work to a system prioritising the people they want to make contact with. Personally, I have developed a huge network with over 10 000 contacts throughout Australia, New Zealand and the United States—the bulk of these people I have met in the last four years during my speaking engagements. I have not kept in touch with everyone of them every 90 days. The 'spheres of influence' (refer to page 48) hear from me most regularly and I hear from them most regularly.

As my resources and my database continue to grow, more of my newsletters will be produced and mailed to more and more contacts. Having a master plan is extremely important in the networking environment.

In the ideal world, with unlimited resources, who would you make contact with and what would you send them?

# 6

# *What do I do at a networking function?*

This chapter will explain to you how to attend a networking function, move out of your comfort zone and have fun—all at the same time, as well as have quality conversations, give out business cards and maybe even walk away with business.

What is a networking function? Any function or get together where, preferably, there are at least five people who you don't yet know. Some networking functions are informal—for example, football club, tennis club, parents and citizens groups. Some are more structured—for example, Lions Club, Rotary, Toastmasters International, chambers of commerce.

At some networking groups there are regular members and you will know everyone—how well do you know them? The biggest trap in this situation is that we sit in the same place time after time and get to know a small clique really well. Three quarters of the people in the room are just names and faces to us. Again, we have to move out of that comfort zone and sit with people we don't know very well in order to keep expanding our networks all the time. Networking really becomes a lifestyle, not something we only do when we want something from others.

Back in the 1980s cold calling or making contact with people we did not know was the way most salespeople went about selling their product or service. The degree to which they knew the prospect determined whether it was a cold, warm or hot call. Largely, though, selling in the 1980s was about talking to enough strangers until you found someone who wanted your product.

Networking has definitely replaced the need for cold calling. Take the banking profession as an example. Unless you consider someone who has joined the banking profession in the last two years, the situation was that they did not apply for a sales position—they applied for a non-sales position in the banking profession. Today, every position in the banking profession involves sales, whether it is a teller, business development manager or customer service position. All staff are now conscious of the sales focus.

Networking takes all the sales pressure off these people. If they regularly attend networking functions, they don't have to cold call. They simply follow up the people they meet at networking functions. More often than not, the person has already had a whinge to them about what their current bank is doing or not doing.

Many professional people are not 'salespeople'. However, most of their firms and companies must now have a sales and marketing focus to perform in today's competitive market. The great news for these professions is that networking replaces cold calling as they knew it, and had also come to fear it. Imagine a banker attending a chamber of commerce function, introducing themselves to, say, the local electrician. The electrician makes a comment that he banks with X Bank. Fine, the banker is not trying to steal customers. She merely makes the comment that if X Bank ever lets him down to call her. They may be able to help him. Or she may ask if there is anything X Bank is not doing that he would like them to do.

Many non-salespeople try to compete with businesses when they don't know what they are competing with. Until you know what your competitor is doing, you can't compete on equal footing. You need to know as much about your competition as you do about your own business, otherwise you can't compete.

Taking the time to attend at least one networking function every week is great for business development. Here you will find unlimited opportunities to network and allow your business to grow through helping others to grow theirs.

In the networking environment, if you can help people get what they want, they will help you get what you want. The law of reciprocity tells us that what we give away comes back ten-fold. Networking triggers this chain reaction, we give away something and something indirectly or directly comes back to us.

True networkers climb up the ladder of success and when they get to the top of it, throw down more ladders to help their friends with their climb to the top.

Some people get to the top of the ladder and throw the ladder away so that no one else will ever share their success—these people do not value their networks, nor are they good networkers. Other people get to the top of the ladder and realise they have been leaning against the wrong wall all the time—these people need to network.

## Which functions will I go to?

Attending networking functions creates an opportunity for you to meet and mingle with like-minded people. First, you must do your research on what groups are appropriate for you.

Make a list of five people in your current network who you believe are successfully growing their business.

1. _____
2. _____
3. _____
4. _____
5. _____

Make a note in your diary as to a time to make contact with these people by phone or fax to ask them what networks they currently attend. More importantly, in their opinion, what networks would they recommend that you attend. Don't be afraid to *ask for help*.

*continued ...*

At the same time, don't waste people's time asking for leads you will never use. Most successful people are busy and appreciate calls where you come straight to the point, ask questions succinctly and don't waffle on about the weather. Role play your planned conversation or make a list of the questions you want to ask. Always enquire, 'Have I caught you at a bad time? I wanted to ask you two quick questions.' You are then showing that you respect their time and their opinion as well as giving them an out if it is a difficult time for them.

In the networking environment, everyone knows that sooner or later they will all need help themselves so they are more than happy to help you if they can. For example, John asked Mary for help in recommending a good physiotherapist. Mary has never needed a physio, but knows that Jill goes to one. Mary puts John in touch with Jill and assistance is given. Win–win all around.

**KEY POINT**

*If you always aim to create a win–win situation with every encounter you have, you will quickly be regarded as a true networker.*

This principle is extremely important when you are attending networking functions. Some people make the mistake of seeing 50 or more people in a room and immediately pounce on the people that they think will do instant business with them. It is preferable to think of the first two or three times you attend the same group as a 'getting to know you/you getting to know me' period. Take the focus off what you are promoting and look at who you can do business with.

More than likely, with this attitude you will actually walk away with business on your third appearance at this group. Many people attend a networking group once, walk away with no business and never go back. It is important to gradually build your profile at the same group month after month rather than attending five different groups once each and achieving nothing.

Some people attend the ideal networking group for them, get really excited at the opportunities, join on the night and then never go back. A year later when it is renewal time, they don't renew because they did not receive any business from the group. People can only do business with you if they have met you personally, been referred to you, or get to know you over a period of time.

Don't join any group unless you are committed to attend at least one function per month. Otherwise, it is more beneficial financially just to pay the extra charge for non-members at the functions you do attend.

What networking functions do you currently attend? _____

What groups are you or your company currently members of? _____

How often do you attend functions with these
organisations or associations? _____

Are you getting value from your memberships?     Yes               No
(circle your response)

When renewal time comes around for these     Yes               No
memberships, could you consider joining other
groups?

What other networking functions are available in your area or have been
recommended to you? _____

*Name*                                               *Phone/contact*

*continued ...*

Now make a note in your diary to attend a number of networking groups in the coming 90 days. Phone today and check times and venues and ask to be put on the mailing list. Most groups will keep you on the mailing list for at least three months and only delete your name if you have not attended any functions during that time.

A list of many of the networking groups available can be found in *The Australian Women's Directory*, edited by Kay Healy and available from Pearlfisher Publications, 226 Darling Street, Balmain, Sydney, ph: (02) 9810 4101, fax: (02) 9810 6024. This book contains groups as diverse as arts, media and publishing through to university services and associations.

Another good source of what's on is the local and daily papers. Smart networkers combine their interests with their networking. One successful banker attends three different gyms each week to spread his networking activity. Another, a successful real estate agent, works a four-day week and spends two days on the golf course—an endless supply of referrals for her.

What are your interests? _____

Can you combine networking with any of these interests? If so, how? _____

Many people make the mistake of dividing their work and pleasure time as networking and non-networking, when these areas comfortably overlap. More business is happening in the social environment than ever before. Remember, it is not who you know but who knows you.

## Tips for attending networking functions

1. Remember to take your business cards with you and use them. Practise introducing yourself and handing your business card out as part of your introduction: 'Hi, I'm John Thirst, I am a business development manager with X Bank.' That's it as far as you mentioning the bank. Your card says it all.

2. The best networkers are also the best listeners. Ask questions and listen to the answers. Focus on the answers rather than on who else is in the room. Make eye contact with the person you are speaking to.

3. Take a supply of blank cards in case you meet people without their business cards.

4.  Introduce yourself to the organiser/president/convenor. Ask questions about the group and, of course, show interest in the answers.

5.  Take two pens. Someone at your table may want to take notes. It is even better if the pen is a promotional tool for your company/business.

6.  Move out of your comfort zone. Sit with people you don't know rather than the 'old faithfuls' you have known for years.

7.  If it is a sit-down function (e.g. breakfast or lunch) introduce yourself as the table fills. If there are 10 people at the table, pass around nine cards. Three people will be relieved that you started giving out cards, three people will think you are pushy (that's okay) and three people will curse themselves for not bringing their own cards.

8.  Always register for attending the function ahead of time. Pre-pay for your ticket if possible. You will earn lots of gold stars with the organisers if you register and pre-pay early.

9.  Prepare an introduction that allows you to present yourself in less than 10 words. One of the skills of networking is being remembered positively. If your introduction drags on too long, people switch off and stop listening.

10. Don't just show up unannounced and expect a meal or seat to be provided for you. Treat people as you would like to be treated.

11. Keep your eye out for first timers. These people often look and feel like a fish out of water. Making the first contact with these people can often endear you to them for life. Think back to the first time you attended a group that you now regularly attend. Were you nervous, uncomfortable, wishing the floor would swallow you up? Did this feeling of panic pass once someone spoke to you? Every best friend was once a total stranger.

12. Prepare two or three questions that you can comfortably ask total strangers (see Chapter 7, Conversation starters).

13. Always check the dress code. Dress to match the highest ranking person in the room. Most business networks happen before or after work. You are better to be over than underdressed.

14. *If you are a first timer at networking functions—don't panic!* Take a number of deep breaths. Repeat to yourself 'every best friend was initially a total stranger'. Look for the friendly faces as well as the people who look as lost as you do. You've paid your money, make the most of it, talk to someone— anyone—and be positive.

## When can you attend your first/next networking function?

Look at your diary now and decide when you have free time to attend a networking function in the next month. Breakfast, lunch, dinner, mid-week, weekend. When are you free? Once you have the time slot, ask friends and associates what is available at that time that would fulfil your needs and move you out of your comfort zone.

There is really no excuse for anyone in business—or anyone wanting to be in business—for not attending networking functions today. There are many international groups that have been around for years—for example, Toastmasters International, Zonta Club, Business and Professional Women, Lions Club, Rotary Club International, chambers of commerce, SWAP (Salespeople With A Purpose) as well as associations, sporting groups and special interest groups. Over the last five years, as the whole networking message has spread, there has been a huge growth in networking groups. East Coast Business Women's Network (covering Queensland, New South Wales and

Victoria) was formed in 1993. Business Enterprise Centres are in most regional areas in Australia. As well as the many *Friends of* … in the art and cultural areas. Checking the yellow pages under 'associations and clubs' will give you some idea of what is available.

### KEY POINT

*Go to a networking function at least once a week. Make it easy for people to do business with you. Always follow up with the people you meet.*

# 7

# Conversation starters

## What do I say after 'hello'?

Having moved you out of your comfort zone and gotten you to a networking function in the previous chapters, this chapter will now give you some tips on making conversation with perfect strangers. A personality and the ability to communicate clearly are prerequisites for successful networking.

## Golden rules for networking functions

○  Listen, listen, listen.

○  Be friendly.

○  Make eye contact.

○  Smile.

○  Act interested.

○  Observe body language—crossed arms, lack of eye contact indicate a lack of interest.

○  Befriend first-timers.

○  Ask open-ended questions—that is, questions requiring more than a 'yes' or 'no' answer.

○ Read the paper or listen to the latest news prior to arriving. You will at least be able to pass an opinion on any current topic.

○ Don't fear pauses when you make conversation. Most people dislike pauses and will jump in with conversation to fill the space.

○ Be positive.

## Questions to ask at networking functions

1. If you introduce yourself to a current member of the group:

   (a) What has been the main benefit you have received from being a member of this group?

   (b) What is the criteria for membership?

   (c) How many members does the club have?

   (d) How long has this group been operating?

2. What's your opinion of the election result? (Play safe on hot topics. Find out which camp they are in before you start preaching your opinion.)

3. What was the highlight of your day? weekend? last week? Don't focus on negative topics. Keep your conversation light and interesting.

4. Have you seen the movie, the play, read the book …? Often if we reveal a little about our interests we find common ground.

5. I'm planning a holiday in … and I'm hoping to get some tips on must sees, do you know anyone who has ever been there?

6. I'm buying a new …, where did you buy yours? Would you shop there again?

7. What tips would you give someone who has never attended one of these functions before?

8. I'm driving to … this evening, do you know anyone who will be heading in that direction tonight and may need a lift?

9. Can you tell me who the organiser of this function is? I would like to compliment them on a great night.

10. How long have you been coming to these functions?

11. If I could arrange to grant you one wish this week, what would it be?

12. What would your ideal client look like? I may already know someone who could do business with you.

# The power of listening

Remember, ask questions and then listen. Make notes on their business card if you plan to follow up. Don't be afraid to introduce yourself to strangers. Recently, my flight from Auckland was delayed and I struck up a conversation with a fellow traveller in the Koru Club lounge of the Air New Zealand terminal. I spoke to this gentleman for around 20 minutes before his own flight was boarding. In that 20 minutes, I asked him five questions (using no more than 50 words total). All of the questions were about him and his business and the conversation flowed as he shared many things about his business, his family, his plans for the future.

For the bulk of the 20 minutes, I listened, made eye contact and asked relevant questions. My total contribution to the exchange was less than 80 words in all. As he left the Koru Club Lounge to board his flight he said, 'Robyn, you are one of the most interesting people I have met this year.' I thanked him for his compliment and grinned to myself realising that all I did was listen to someone talk enthusiastically about their life. That's what made me interesting. I asked questions and I listened. Why not try it yourself with the next stranger you meet.

Some people are so nervous making conversation with strangers that they don't listen at all, rather they concentrate on what their next question will be and, as a result, the conversation does not flow. Everyone was a 'first-timer' once at a networking function. We've all been there. Just relax and try to enjoy yourself.

Don't jump to conclusions—avoid making unwarranted assumptions about what the person is going to say or mentally trying to complete their sentence. Don't interrupt—only prisoners like to be interrupted in the middle of their sentence. A pause—even a long pause—doesn't always mean they are finished saying what they wanted.

Try to talk to people about non-work related topics. Eighty per cent of the population does not get recognition on the job. Many people do not want to talk about their job. Find out what puts a sparkle in their eyes, and talk about that. Take the focus off you and put it on to them—you will be pleasantly surprised at the results. Ask yourself, out of all the people in the room, why would someone want to speak to me?

### KEY POINTS

*Ask questions and listen to the answers.*

*Maintain eye contact while the person is speaking to you.*

*Limit your own talking.*

# 8

# *Be seen, get known, move ahead*

## How to raise your profile positively

This chapter will explain the importance of, first, being remembered and, second, being remembered positively. There is no point networking if you constantly create a negative impression.

Why is it that out of two people who regularly attend a function, one gets known really quickly and the other barely has their name acknowledged by a handful of people? Does shyness have anything to do with it? Is one person pushy while the other is quiet?

In the networking environment, the people who are remembered are those who:

O   follow up when they say they will;

O   refer business to others regularly;

O   promise good, deliver great;

O   connect people with people they can do business with;

O    share information generously; and

O   believe in the networking concept that there is plenty for everyone—plenty of business, plenty of money, plenty of opportunities, plenty of ideas. Maybe all of these are not in your possession now, but they could be one day.

## Generating referrals

These people—who are easily remembered—are known as *spheres of influence*. They are not born this way, they become it. In the old days when companies were over-staffed, one of the classic spheres of influence was the tea lady. The tea lady knew everything about everyone. People talked to these people and freely shared information. In today's busy world, the spheres of influence are not necessarily the chief executive officers or managing directors. Spheres of influence often hold the lower ranks within a company.

I was asked recently in a radio interview whether networkers were born or made. My reply was born networkers are spheres of influence and fit the above description. Other people can learn how to network, practise their skills, and ultimately become spheres of influence. What an exciting world we will live in when everyone embraces this concept and freely gives information, business, leads, resources, assets—the works.

Spheres of influence are the people who many companies try to attract to endorse their products. Spheres of influence always work with integrity and can rarely been seen endorsing something or someone they do not believe in. So what would it take to make you a sphere of influence and build a positive profile in your company or your community?

Based on the previous chapters, we have read that great networkers:

O give out and, ideally, exchange 50 business cards each week;

O send a thank you card per day, often to non-work related people; and

O attend at least one networking function every week.

To this list we could add the following points.

## Referrals

*Refer one piece of business to someone every day*: Become known for the number of referrals you make. Explain clearly to the person receiving the referral, first, that you expect them to do their personal best for this person and, second, that you expect them to get back to you and let you know how it goes. If these two criteria are not met, find another person who values your referrals more.

If you refer business to someone who you have met socially but have never done business with, mention this to the person requesting a referral. It is important to cover your good name always. Ask that person to get back to you also and let you know how it went. Many businesses that are dependent on referrals find their referral sources dry up and they wonder why. In Chapter 1, I spoke about the power of referring business and the potential dollar value to your business. Each time you receive a referral, you need to have a system in place to thank that person. Whether it's a fax, a phone call, a bunch of flowers, a bottle of wine, a magazine subscription—whatever seems appropriate for the size of the referral. There needs to be a system in place.

I recently polled a group of people (100) on whether they would prefer a written or a verbal thank you for giving a referral. Ninety seven per cent preferred the written thank you. Written thank yous are placed on the notice board, shown to other people, remembered. If 99 per cent of your business could come from referrals, wouldn't it be worth having a system in place to acknowledge these gifts? Referrals are gifts. They were given to you freely. Again, this is where having stationery supplies on hand to assist with this system is very important. Add a page to your list of company procedures: 'Follow these steps for every referral received', and then list how you want referrals to be acknowledged. As your business grows, each staff member reads the book of procedures. This need only be half a dozen pages. Can you imagine the potential of whole companies working the one system of giving regular recognition to their customers? (See Chapter 9 for a more detailed discussion of recognition.)

Another key with referrals is not to waste time asking for them if you have no intention of using them. Some people spend all their time collecting referrals and then never follow up. Don't waste people's time—again, a real no-no for networking.

## Committee positions

We all know you don't have any spare time, no one does. However, it is you who wants to raise your profile and become a shining light in your sea of competitors. Become involved in a committee that you are genuinely interested in—it may be sport, the arts, the environment, the political arena, wherever your interests lie. In the short term you may just offer to help out on the registration desk, or the meeting and greeting. Wear a name tag, introduce yourself to others, find out how you can help people. If they are seeking assistance in fund raising, who do you know who may be able to donate something? You don't have to do it for the rest of your life—who knows, you may even enjoy it. More importantly you are networking with decision-makers and people who are making it happen and know other people who are making it happen out there.

## Promotional material

Develop a win–win relationship with your printer. It is important that your letterhead, with compliments slip, business cards etc. reflect the image you are wanting to create. If you are starting out in business and your budget is not huge, meet with a reliable printer who can discuss an entire range of items with you and, as your business grows, you can introduce more items to your promotional material.

When you are out networking, you will meet lots of people who may be interested in your products or services one day, but not today. You want to have a brochure or a good quality and inexpensive flyer that you can send them. Many people make the mistake of having a fantastic promotional package that has cost the earth to produce (plus courier or mail out costs) and they are reluctant to send them out because they cost so much. As a result they don't send them out, no one knows what a great service they have and the brochures sit on the shelf and become obsolete.

Get feedback from people (friends and strangers alike) who will tell you quite honestly the message your promotional material conveys. Is this congruent with the message you are wanting to give? Are you fun loving and carefree and yet have very conservative promotional material? Are you giving mixed messages? It is best to ask the opinion of people who do not have a vested interest in the material.

## Birthdays

Birthdays are generally fun days. Even if we don't want to grow old, our birthday is our special day. Remembering clients' birthdays is frowned on in some professions. Maybe so, yet I send on average 10 birthday cards a week to people in my networks and some of my clients. To date no one has rung to tell me it is not appropriate—and I keep receiving referrals and repeat business from these people. Maybe we need to take the conservatism out of some of our business practices. Christmas is for everyone, birthdays are your day.

How do you find out when a person's birthday is? Ask them. Many businesses require people to fill out application forms etc., where they list their date of birth—you already have access to this. Alternatively, you can ask them: 'When is your birthday?' Please note, birthday, *not* date of birth. Some people are very guarded about their age, however they will happily reveal their birthday.

The birthday system I use is very simple. I have an old diary and when I find out someone's birthday, I write it down there. Once a week or once a month, depending on my free time, I write birthday cards for those special people that week. I generally use inexpensive cards and then enclose confetti or little stars in the envelope. If I have done the cards weeks ahead, I will write, in pencil, the date each card needs to be posted. The recipients always ring to tell me the inserts went all over the floor or their desk. People don't care how much you know until they know how much you care. There is not enough fun in the workplace, maybe our fun cards can brighten up their work day. Many professionals are fearful of doing things that have not been done before, purely because they will be the first. Be a dare devil—send a birthday card to one client on their special day and see what happens.

## Doing the unexpected and being remembered positively

Around Melbourne Cup time last year, I was working with a banking group in a small Victorian town. For those readers who have never heard of the Melbourne Cup, it is an annual horse race which is held in Melbourne on the first Tuesday in November. Apart from the huge prize money for the winner, there is a big day of celebration and, in many parts of Australia, lunches, fashion parades and all sorts of celebrations are held on that day, prior to the race which is run mid-afternoon. There are generally 20 plus horses in the race.

My suggestion to this banking group was to select 20 plus top clients (depending on the number of starters in the race) and phone these top clients on the day of the race. Advise their customers that they had just run a sweep (a competition based on the horses in the race) and that client had drawn such and such a horse. Now, if that horse comes first, they will win dinner for two at a restaurant, second place will win a bunch of flowers, third place will win a bottle of champagne (prizes will be dependent on the budget available). The company running the sweep would, of course, say this was a complimentary sweep because they were VIP clients and their business was highly valued.

Let me tell you, the bankers I was working with looked at me like I had two heads and was speaking in a foreign language. They had never done this before and wondered if it was appropriate for their profession.

I am pleased to say that two of those sceptical bankers took up my challenge and ran a sweep for their clients and it was a huge success. Even the clients whose horses didn't win a prize talked about it for weeks. Had their bank ever done this before? No. Will they do this again next year? I hope so.

Don't be afraid to do the things that haven't been done before in your industry. The fact they have not been done before does not mean they won't work.

Again, one bank took up on my idea of giving an Easter egg to everyone who made a deposit on Easter Thursday. This small gift did not break the bank's budget and certainly cheered up a lot of customers on that day.

Retailers can do the same thing. One newsagent I know has Monday as his 'red frog day'. Anyone who makes a purchase over $3 gets a red frog (a type of sweet). He is located in a central business area and, of course, it is not surprising that Monday is one of his busiest days. As another example, a boutique I know does not discount clothing. However, it has a sliding scale and when anyone purchases garments over $250, they include a complimentary pair of earrings, over $500 and a scarf or belt is included.

A restaurant gives a free lunch to anyone having a birthday (of course, with documentation to prove this). Do you think many people celebrate their

*Be seen, get known, move ahead*

birthdays alone? Not usually, the record is a booking for 25 people—all from one complimentary meal. Simple ideas that positively increase the profile of the people or the business. None of these ideas costs much and the results they achieve are remarkable.

## Faxes

Faxes are another great keep-in-touch idea. A one page sheet that includes a cartoon or an article you have read in a magazine or newspaper is a great way of keeping in touch. With a handwritten note such as: 'Hi Joe, saw this and thought of you!' can have quite an impact. Faxes are also great because the recipient can look at it in their own time. Make sure the fax doesn't run more than one page. Many people have an aversion to companies sending reams of pages of useless information. If you can't get your message across on one page, ask someone for help to reduce your message.

Be aware that faxes are generally public domain. Don't put anything on a fax that may embarrass the person receiving it or anything that you feel the person would not want others to see.

## E-mail

As discussed in Chapter 3, E-mail has opened up many doors in the communication world. We are living in such exciting times when we can communicate with people on the other side of the world in a matter of seconds. It is mind boggling when you think of what the future in communications may hold.

## Postcards

Some people have a general postcard that they use for all networking correspondence, thank yous, congratulations, how's things? etc. Postcards do work quite effectively in that you have a limited space to write your message, your company details can appear at the bottom of the card, you save on envelope costs, and your message stands out from the other daily mail. The front of the card may be a photographic design, cartoon or line drawing depending on the type of company or person you are promoting.

I use travel postcards to keep in touch with my clients. I may be attending a conference in the United States, New Zealand or Asia and I will select a local postcard and share with a client an idea that I have seen or heard that may be appropriate for their business. Of course, I write that I will give them a call on my return to discuss further. I normally take 10 or 15 addressed labels for which ever clients I want to make contact with that month. That way, when I do see something suitable for them, I jot a card in a couple of minutes. As with the birthday cards, I have not had negative feedback about my postcards.

## Newspaper articles

Newspaper articles were mentioned briefly earlier. International and interstate newspapers are available at all capital city airports and many five star hotels. At least once a week I buy international papers, to keep me up to date with global trends. I then cut these papers to pieces and usually keep some on my files and send selected articles to members of my network or clients with a handwritten note such as: 'Thought this may interest you.' There is a possibility they will have read it also, that's okay. However, it is more than likely that they have not read it and will be impressed that you don't just think of them when you are after an order. This is the biggest mistake sales people make—only contacting customers when you want them to place an order. You will never hope to build a relationship with this attitude. Keeping in touch with clients, finding a reason to contact them—the result is that you never have to ask for an order because they ring you.

All of the above ideas help you to build the networking bridge and put another link in the networking chain. Each time we make non-work related contact with someone, our links grow stronger and stronger. We are constantly developing trust and earning respect. Networking is really the glue that keeps relationships together.

# 9

# *The power of recognition*

This chapter will discuss one of the most important keys to networking—that is, giving recognition. If we can master giving recognition to ourselves as well as to others, we will achieve unlimited networking success.

In previous chapters we have touched on the importance of giving recognition, wowing our customers and showing that we value their current business and their potential to refer clients to us.

## How important is recognition to you?

Unless you are living on a desert island, recognition is probably extremely important to you, as it is to most people today. It is also one of the single most important things missing in many people's lives. In Australia, if you were born in the 1950s you were given the title of 'baby boomers' and this is a whole marketing niche that many companies have successfully marketed to. Anyone born in the 1950s, or even prior to this, were more than likely not encouraged to blow their own trumpets or sing their own praises. Rather they were taught to 'be seen and not heard', 'promote others before you promote yourself' and to stand at the back of the line always.

For some entrepreneurial baby boomers now, it is a challenge to discard these childhood and teen-years belief systems. As it is for the entrepreneur who decides to go into business for themselves and become the 'boss'. This 'boss' often turns out to be the toughest boss they have ever had—they give themselves no recognition, little positive input and beat up on themselves all the time. Even worse, if it is a home based business (certainly a growth market in the 90s) they can fall into the trap of working very long hours and never getting out of the house. For these people, networking at least once a week is critical.

Networking groups tend to attract people who want to break out of that negative mould and run successful businesses themselves, or have successful careers as employees. Most of us beat up on ourselves daily for what we didn't do, rather than acknowledging our achievements—what we did accomplish (see Chapter 5 on time management).

If we admit to beating up on ourselves like this, chances are our staff and our customers will do the same. So what can we do to change this pattern, to encourage positive thought and give ourselves and others regular recognition?

Figure 9.1 Recognition

## How important is recognition to:

❑ You

❑ Your staff

❑ Your clients

**How can you give your clients RECOGNITION this week?**

## Keeping a success log

A success log can be a two-line entry in the bottom of your diary page, acknowledging your 'win' or 'success' for the day. Maybe you got through two items on your 'to do' list, maybe you completed a difficult assignment, handled a difficult customer—no matter how small it was, you had a win. If we start to record our wins every day (large and small) we will be taking the first step in valuing ourselves.

Low self-esteem is prevalent in all walks of life in today's competitive society. Our self-talk (the endless radio that plays in our heads) determines the fluctuation levels of our daily self-esteem levels and often the success of the day. What does this remotely have to do with networking? Plenty, believe me.

Can you imagine what a person would look like standing before you with 10 out of 10 self-esteem—confident, straight back, glint in their eyes, smiling, radiating positivity?

Now a person with 6 out of 10 self-esteem—eyes darting around the room, slightly hunched, not much of a smile, looking a little too unsure and uncomfortable. A person with 3 out of 10 or less self-esteem—no eye contact at all, head bent, radiating overall negativity and very uncomfortable.

At every networking function you attend, you will find all three groups represented. Depending on how you feel at that time this will largely determine which group you will sit with or be attracted to. Like attracts like. Recall the last time you struck up a conversation with someone who was negative, you may have come away feeling so drained because sometimes their negativity is contagious.

Sometimes you can snap people out of their negativity by sharing a humorous story or asking them about themselves. Other times that negative cloud hangs over them all day. They will be the people who always complain about the queues, the food, the speaker, the air conditioning, the parking, their day, their boss, their partner, their children—their life is one big complaint. Not surprisingly, these people are often left in the corner to be miserable by themselves at a networking function.

In Chapter 7, one of the questions was: What was the highlight of your day? Persist when you ask this question as it is surprising how often we focus on the negative. Personally, I try to avoid the negative people at networking functions because you waste a lot of time trying to cheer them up when they are happy being negative. Ideally, introduce one negative person to another, then they can enjoy each other's negative company.

The success log is step one in giving yourself recognition. The second step may be having a poster on the wall where you record your 'Wins for the Year' and when you achieve what you think was a win, write it down. Yes, you will risk other people reading your wins—that's okay. How can people give you recognition when they don't know what you have done?

We are great at dismissing our successes. Someone phones us to congratulate us on something we did weeks ago, and we dismiss it saying 'Oh that, that was nothing' and move on to what is happening now. At a number of the networking groups such as the East Coast Business Women's Network and SWAP, there is a segment where members and guests are encouraged to share their wins for the week or month. It is amazing at times, how sensational some of these wins are. Had we not asked people to share their wins, no one would have been any the wiser. Some of the wins included: securing a major government contract; being a finalist in the Small Business Awards; completing an M.B.A.; getting married; getting promotions; buying a first home; the list went on—all major wins, and had we not asked, no recognition would have been given.

## Success log in the workplace

With many of the corporate clients I work with, I suggest that they have a success log or 'win' system in place. At least once a week, preferably at the end of each day, a small group of employees get together and quickly share their 'win' with the group. No matter how bad the day has been, the small slice of recognition is what that person takes home with them.

In one real estate office I know of, there is a trophy for the person who has taken the latest listing. This enables everyone in the office to have the trophy on their desk at some stage. Encouragement is then given to the high achievers as well as the less successful agents, who one day may join the ranks of high achievers. In one telemarketing department, a bell is rung everytime a sale is made. Simple systems that encourage and support recognition in the workplace.

How do you give yourself recognition?

Daily:

Weekly:

Yearly:

If you do not have any systems in place at present, what could you do (within your budget) to give yourself recognition?

Some of the recognition rewards I have observed people use include: weekly massage; mini holidays; weekends away; movies; plays; walks along the beach;

the afternoon off to do nothing; a drive in the country; shopping; dancing; quality time with your children or partner; a night out; or time out to read and relax. Is there something one of your associates rewards themselves with that you would like to do also? What is stopping you?

People often say 'money' is the answer to the above question. Reality is that in the networking world, there are unlimited opportunities to barter your services. Maybe you could mind someone else's children and they reciprocate. You may swap houses with someone for the long weekend—even staying on the opposite side of the city can be an interesting experience. You can do someone's typing if they will do your accounts—the possibilities are endless. The most important message here is to give yourself regular recognition.

> How will you give yourself recognition this week?
>
> Which of your products or services could you barter this week?
>
> Who would you like to barter with? Do you know anyone who knows this person or company?

## How important is recognition to your staff?

Again, it is extremely important that whether your staff are casual or full-time workers, everyone wants to know they have done a good job and, more importantly, that they are appreciated. Many companies make the mistake of only rewarding the sales staff with incentives and bonuses. In reality, if the sales people did not have the support of the back office/factory people, the orders would not get out in the first place. Smart companies these days are valuing their entire staff's contribution to their profits.

Employee of the month awards, either nominated by a client or a fellow worker, are gaining in popularity. Often it is not the 'gift' they receive, just the opportunity to be acknowledged for their effort.

## What recognition systems are in place for your staff members?

If there is none at present, what could be introduced? Having a brainstorming session with the staff often produces amazing results. What would they like as a reward? Management are often surprised when the answer is not money. Conditions are often more important to staff members. An afternoon off to go shopping, an extended lunch hour, a later start or earlier finish—these answers are often the result of these brainstorming sessions. Giving all your staff members business cards is often the quickest way to boost their self-esteem and give them recognition. Encourage all staff to give away business cards to their friends and relations. All staff members have networks, some very diverse to management's. From these networks, business can evolve. Most firms have business sitting under their nose through the contacts their staff have and yet they spend thousands of dollars looking outside their businesses for leads. Tapping into their internal networks is a great way of growing their businesses.

| | | |
|---|---|---|
| Do you have any systems in place to encourage staff to bring business to the company? | Yes | No |
| If so, what are they? Do they need a revamp? | Yes | No |
| If not, could you arrange a brainstorming session with the staff to discuss an incentive system? | Yes | No |

### How important is recognition to your customer?

Recognition is probably as important to you as it is to your customer—extremely important. Would you think many chief executive officers or general managers receive recognition from their staff? The research I have done shows this is a rare event in most boardrooms. Pats on the back are uncommon. Yet these people, too, want recognition.

This is where reading newspapers and magazines and being up on local events is very important. Your clients may be going through major changes in their industry, through deregulation, takeovers, mergers or new competitors. It is important that you are aware of what is happening in your marketplace. Keeping in touch with your clients every 90 days (as discussed in previous chapters) is very important. A quick fax offering encouragement or support for a stand they may have taken or a new product they have introduced can really endear yourself to them.

Caring about their business is also important. Knowing what their competitors are doing and how market trends are affecting their business can help you to advise them or alter your product to suit their needs.

### New Australian niche markets

An example of a new niche market is the single person household in Australia—part of a growing demographic with special needs. A study commissioned by

First National Real Estate in early 1995 found that there are 1.4 million single occupant homes representing about one in five households, or 10 per cent of the population. We are now seeing the disappearance of negative stereotypes surrounding singles. Old trends would have described a single person as aged under 26 and unmarried, whereas now more and more singles are in their late 30s and 40s.

The major banks, which once spurned loan applications from single people, are now targeting singles with major packages offering low interest loans, credit cards and bank fee exemptions. Bankers and real estate managers should know that singles are the market niche of the future and that this is the area where marketing dollars must be spent. Single people also have different dietary requirements. They would not necessarily buy large economy anything, rather they would look at the smallest serves available of some items to reduce wastage.

How does this niche market affect your client base? If you were supplying packaging to the food industry, your clients' requirements would change dramatically. It is important, both for the growth of your business and the success of your clients' business, to stay up to date on marketing trends.

Five years ago, we would never have expected to receive soup and bread roll on a short domestic flight between capital cities. This is commonplace now and has been very well received by the regular traveller who wants a snack—something light and nutritious. This is a whole new market for pre-packaged hot food. There are endless examples of changes to our eating habits and shopping needs. These changes are impacting on our clients as well as our businesses.

This is often where the guest speakers at the networking functions can share new ideas and concepts in a non-educational environment. Most professional speakers supply handouts at these events and it may be an opportunity for you to share the information you receive here with your client. Remember, great networkers are not afraid to share information, there is plenty of everything for everyone.

---

First, we need to identify who is in our current network. Please list groups of people rather than individuals.

Who is in my current network—for example, relations, work friends?

| | | |
|---|---|---|
| 1. _____ | 4. _____ | |
| 2. _____ | 5. _____ | |
| 3. _____ | 6. _____ | |
| 7. _____ | 9. _____ | |
| 8. _____ | 10. _____ | |

How are you giving regular recognition to your current network?

---

It is often our closest friends who receive the least recognition. We leave them to last in line, often saying, 'John will understand why I did not call him, he knows I am always busy.' Maybe we can look at sharing with this close group of friends just how important they are in our lives. Unfortunately, with many of these people, we never get to do it.

---

Which special person in your life can you make contact with this week? _____

What about your customers who may only buy          Yes          No
once a year, do they also receive regular contact?
(circle your response)

How much is their repeat business worth to you? _____

No. of once-a-year customers × $_____ = $_____ × number of years = $_____

---

Experts vary on whether loyalty can be bought. Certainly the frequent flyer air points programs have hotted up airline competition in Australia. Again, as stated on the customer ladder of loyalty in Chapter 8, if we never lose a customer, our businesses will continue to grow.

If we give regular recognition to our current customers, we won't lose them. It is purely because we take them for granted that they feel unloved and sometimes look elsewhere. Have systems in place to make regular contact. The simpler the system the better. No matter how large the organisation, make people accountable for a certain number of clients. Encourage them to make regular contact with all of their clients. Networking is a powerful concept because it is all about giving recognition on an ongoing basis. The more contact we make with each person in our network the stronger the links between our networks grow. The more we help other people's businesses grow, the more our own businesses grow.

Let's wave a magic wand and imagine for a moment the year 2000 in Australia—it is the Olympic Games and the whole country is in a state of euphoria. Networking is an accepted way of doing business. Successful businesses are sprouting up everywhere, unemployment is down, job sharing is prevalent as win–win solutions are found for every situation. Advertising as we currently know it is changing; companies advertise less because the bulk of their business is gained by referral. Advertising focuses on giving recognition to customers we already have rather than seeking new customers to continue getting it wrong with, just as we are doing now.

There is a sense of optimism in the air, employee appreciation schemes are in place in all companies, no matter how small. The negative thinkers are now in the minority. Is this possible in such a short time? Maybe not, maybe it will take a few more years. Are you reading this book and identifying some of the things you and your company are not doing? If so, take action today. If you can start giving recognition to you first of all, then your staff and finally your customers, your business will grow beyond all your expectations.

### KEY POINT
*Treat others as you would like to be treated.*

# 10

## Notorious networkers

### Tips and stories from the experts

Great networkers are quick to share information, realising that there is plenty of information, customers and opportunities for everyone. While writing this book, I wondered about the many interesting people I had met in my travels and some I had seen in the media. So I asked some of them a few questions as to their success. Their responses follow.

I faxed each respondent and asked them to send me:

○ their current position

○ their past achievements

○ their most important networking tip

○ their favourite networking story.

### Babette Bensoussan

*Current position:* Managing Director of MindShifts, a company she began in 1992.
*Past achievements:* Bachelor of Business (majoring in Marketing and Economics), Master of Business, sole recipient of the SCIP Fellows Award in 1996.
*No. 1 tip:* Always, always carry your business card with you—you will meet the most unlikely people in the most unlikely places!

*Favourite story:* As a member of the Australian Executive Women's Network, I was able to present my own story on my achievements one evening to all attendees. I talked about my business, dreams and beliefs. In the audience was a person who identified with my business comments and we later got together to share our views. Several months later, this person was speaking at a conference with over 250 attendees. During her presentation to this audience, she referred to me, our conversation and the advice I had given her. Now 250 more people knew about me and my business. One networking opportunity led to someone marketing my business to 250 people for no cost. Amazing, isn't it!

### Wayne Burns

*Current position:* National Director, The Millenium Group.

*Past achievements:* Building from scratch with no capital a successful, profitable and dynamic public affairs company; at age 24, being the youngest press secretary in the Federal Ministry (in 1988).

*No. 1 tip:* Always follow up a new contact, a favour or a meeting with a note—keep your name and that of your enterprise in front of those you want to influence.

*Favourite story:* I was once the victim of a networking good intention gone wrong when I was faxed a 'personalised' thank you note, sent, I was told, to me only to thank me for my special contribution to speaking at a seminar. An hour later I received four similiar notes sporting exactly the same wording intended for other people also involved in the seminar.

### Carmel Niland

*Current position:* Managing Director, Carmel Niland & Associates.

*Past achievements:* Established, as coordinator of NSW Women's unit in 1977, the first network lunch for women and helped establish the spokeswomen network in New South Wales government. Founding member of Women and Management.

*No. 1 tip:* Give without expectation in networking—though it always comes back to you manifold.

*Favourite story:* My favourite story happens in that haven for women's networking—the ladies loo. I was talking to my friend in another cubicle saying 'If only we could get the Premier to come to speak.' As we moved to the washbasin the Premier's wife emerged from the third cubicle saying 'I'll fix it tonight. He'll be there for sure.' Whenever I mention this story to other women I find that they have all got a women's room story.

### Chris Nolan

*Current position:* Managing Director, Nolan O'Rourke & Co. Pty Ltd.

*Past achievements:* Voted Father of the Universe by five children. Wife abstained.

*No. 1 tip:* Take an active role in trade associations relevant to your industry.

*Favourite story:* A young graduate is being presented with his practising certificate by the President of the Institution of Engineers (Aust.), who also is the CEO of one of the largest consulting engineering firms in the country.

'And what do you do?' asked the President.

'Well, actually, I work for you!' he replies having started that same day.

The next day every one of the 750 employees of the firm knew who he was. The CEO had sent a rocket up every executive because he had not been introduced to his newest, most junior engineer.

### Christine Petersen

*Current position:* Priority Management.

*No. 1 tip:* Without a doubt, pass and collect business cards. Always follow up with a note when you meet an interesting person.

*Favourite story:* My business is a management training company. When at dinner with friends one night, I was relating the challenges managers have in the workplace today. Another guest, whom I had not previously met, suggested I contact a friend of theirs. I did so and it resulted in training 60 people within that person's company. (So many people don't follow through and so lose wonderful opportunities.)

### Peter Scarfo

*Current position:* Real estate agent.

*Past achievements:* Past National President, Sales People With a Purpose (SWAP).

*No. 1 tip:* Always treat everyone with respect and wherever you are, be there!

*Favourite story:* Within one week of completing my real estate licence course I received a call from Greg Tebb (Sales Manager, W. Herrmann Real Estate Pty Ltd). I was asked to go for an interview and was offered the job on the spot. All this came about through my association with SWAP. If you get involved with a group and give a little, it's amazing how it comes back to you 100-fold. SWAP has been the source of most of my friendships, business opportunities, personal growth and fun.

### Nancy Knudsen

*Current position:* Chair and Managing Director of Aircruising Australia Ltd, Knudsen Travel P/L t/a Sydney Express, Asia Express Operations Pty Ltd t/a Asia Express.

*No. 1 tip:* Unless you are a used car salesperson, the value of your networking is only as good as your accompanying integrity, and the respect that you have earned in your industry. How often have you heard 'nice guy, but ...'.

*Favourite story:* When I was in my teens, I worked with a tall, slim and very shy person called Joanna Black (name changed) in a large company. Years after I left the company, she became famous by winning a beauty contest and going on to become a very successful photographic model. I wrote and wished her well, and then lost track of her because I moved away. Many years later, her name came up again as she was running a highly successful PR and training firm. I was completely impressed by her versatility, and when I had to contact her through business, wrote a little note saying something like 'Remember me?—congratulations on all your successes.' As she lived in another State, I continued to communicate by small notes on business correspondence from time to time, and we again became quite good friends which helped to further our business interests as well. I was delighted to be doing business with someone who I had known for such a long time. We finally scheduled to meet at a conference that we were both attending. On the appointed day, an unfamiliar short blonde woman approached me. 'Nancy,' she said, 'I am *not* the Joanna Black who you thought I was when you first contacted me, but I have never gathered the courage to tell you. I enjoyed your encouragement so much, and then we were getting on so well, I didn't want to spoil it!' Yes, we are still good friends, yes, we are still doing business, and we both often laughingly wonder what happened to that other Joanna Black.

## Peter Langford

*Current position:* Completing a PhD (on networking!) and MBA at Macquarie University. Teaching in Organisational Psychology at Macquarie University.
*Past achievements:* Skydiving, abseiling, triathlons, consulting and teaching in organisational psychology, surviving postgraduate studies at university ... living!
*No. 1 tip:* Think long term! Real relationships (the most useful and the most fulfilling) take time.
*Favourite story:* The benefits from networking are often completely unpredictable. A couple of years ago I joined the National Speakers Association of Australia. At the first meeting I attended, Robyn Henderson was being given a hearty pat on the back for the immense amount of effort she was putting into developing her speaking career. At that time I had absolutely zero idea that I'd be doing a PhD on networking somewhere down the track.

When I eventually began my PhD, Robyn, being one of the best known networkers in Australia, was one of the first people I spoke to. She then introduced me to other people, lent me books on networking, shared her expertise, and introduced me to the East Coast Business Women's Network—all of which have been extremely satisfying and helpful.

## Cyndi Kaplan

*Current position:* Author, speaker, director.
*Past achievements:* Written five books that have been translated into five languages, ran a successful toy company for 15 years.
*No. 1 tip:* Anyone, anywhere, anytime—talk to them!

*Favourite story:* Jogging in Centennial Park I started chatting to a jogger I had not met before and discovered he was none other than the chairman of Channel 9. I didn't have my business card in my jogging shorts, but I introduced myself and sent him one of my books, *There's a Lipstick in my Briefcase.* Very soon I got an interview on the Midday Show. Lesson learnt: never go jogging without your business card, and never without your lipstick on. Always remember it's not what you know that counts, not even who you know, but who knows you. Start jogging!

## Alister Haigh

*Current position:* Joint Managing Director, Haigh's Chocolates Pty Ltd.
*Past achievements:* Married for 10 years and have 3 children. Helped introduce the Easter Bilby to the Australian market.
*No. 1 tip:* Always carry business cards on you that can be written on.
*Favourite story:* I was in Japan showing retailers our new range of products. A person from another company that I was travelling with went to visit a client of theirs. They took our new range and the customer was impressed and requested us to visit them. The next day, we were in their next catalogue without any modifications to the product and it is now approaching 5 per cent of our buisness.

## Benita Collings

*Current position:* Actor, presenter, trainer.
*Past achievements:* State President, National Speakers Association of Australia.
*No. 1 tip:* Always keep a check on a supposed 'old introduction'—check before removing from database.
*Favourite story:* Some time ago I had occasion to ring a person who was on my database to check if they were doing my workshop. As they weren't there, I left a message on their answer phone. I received a call on my answer phone saying to ring. Now, I have two people with exactly the same name on my database, so I rang the 'strange' one first, explained that I had the two names, and was it he who had called. No, it wasn't and, to cut a long story short, although he didn't do my course, I'm now doing training for his company!

## Ron Lee

*Current position:* The Corporate Ninja—Corporate Hoaxer and Executive Trainer.
*No. 1 tip:* Fly Business or First Class.
*Favourite story:* The ARIMA conference keynote hoax had been well received, so I was on a bit of a high. On the flight from Adelaide, I happened to sit beside the State manager of a large pharmaceutical company. We began to banter. We spoke about our occupational concerns and about professional wrestling. Arriving in Sydney, he said that it was his most enjoyable flight ever and wrote two names on his card, insisting that I contact his counterparts. I told him he

showed great faith in an unseen commodity. He said he had a feeling that I'd be just right for their upcoming conference. Thus began a friendship and a valuable relationship with a company.

### Jan Davis

*Current position:* General Manager, Australian Mushroom Growers Association.
*Past achievements:* Maintaining sanity after working in associations for 15 years—although some may question this!
*No. 1 tip:* I always follow up after meeting people: thank you notes, birthday cards, pass on relevant bits of information and so on.
*Favourite story:* On Christmas Day in 1988, I was in Marakesh in Morocco and met some other Australians. We got talking after a few drinks (only a few) and it turned out one of the fellows worked in a field allied to mine. I pulled out the trusty business card (yes, even on holidays!) and went on my way. Two months later, back at the desk, a phone call came in from someone who knew the fellow I'd met in Morocco, offering me a very interesting consultancy on his recommendation.

### Martin Moroney

*Current position:* Discovery Multimedia Productions.
*No. 1 tip:* Robert Kennedy said 'Ask not what your country can do for you. Ask what you can do for your country.' Working in multimedia, a large proportion of people I meet telegraph to me that their first thought on meeting me is what can they get out of me, not what they can do for me. They have taught me that in networking, it's what you can do for people that's important—that's networking with integrity.
*Favourite story:* A colleague was telling me on a flight to Amsterdam about his new neighbour who sold military junk. He thought it was wild that this bloke was currently trying to sell three DC3 Dakotas and a Motor Torpedo Boat.
Later that day on a connecting flight to London I was discussing the ways that people earn their living with the passenger in the next seat. We got round to the subject of the military junk. To my amazement he got really excited and asked how he could contact my friend. You've guessed it, he bought the Motor Torpedo Boat.

### Jenna Ford

*Current position:* Coordinator, Women Making The Difference.
*Past achievements:* Managing Director, Clearways Consulting and Training.
*No. 1 tip:* Networking is not just about who you can link with. It's more about the big picture—that is, who can you link others with as well as including yourself. I call it 'netwebbing'.

*Favourite story:* As part of demonstrating netwebbing, the women at the October 1995 Women Making The Difference seminar wove a vast web of coloured wool across the conference room. On the web they pinned requests for support for a specific project they each had. They all left that day with tangible offers of support, and reports that have since been confirmed, show that many took the offers into action. Get specific when you request netweb support. It works.

## Marita Blood

*Current position:* Managing Director, Marita Blood & Associates.
*No. 1 tip:* Never let people know you are networking.
*Favourite story:* Some time ago a so-called friend of 20 years who had recently gone into the real estate business invited me to her place for dinner. She said, 'The only reason I am inviting you is because of your excellent banking contacts who would be able to let me know what properties are coming on to the market.' I was shocked, but quickly replied, 'The sort of bankers I know only do $100 million commercial property deals.' This story supports my No. 1 networking tip.

## Greg Lenthen

*Current position:* Travel Editor, *Sydney Morning Herald.*
*Past achievements:* Having the celebrated author and speaker Robyn Henderson as a cousin.
*No. 1 tip:* Acquire a skilled networker as a close relation.
*Favourite story:* A professional networker, who shall remain nameless, successfully inveigled other networkers into writing a whole chapter of one of her books. Not surprisingly, the response to the notorious networker's requests was overwhelming. In the true networking spirit, many people were prepared to share their tips and stories hopefully so that others can see how easy it is, as well as gaining from their experience.

Unfortunately, I was unable to include all the responses I received in this chapter. However, we are planning a Notorious Networkers publication in the new year.

# How to run a successful networking function

Why is it that some networking functions are great and others just don't seem to get off the ground? Many organisers think that successful functions just happen. I strongly disagree—we make them happen. In this chapter I would like to discuss some basics for running successful networking functions, regardless of their size.

In earlier chapters we discussed the concept that every person over 21 would know approximately1000 people. Picturing a room with 30 people in it, this then equates to the potential to tap into 30 000 people, though admittedly there may be some overlapping.

## Name tags

It is critical to give total strangers name tags to make it very easy for them to introduce themselves to each other. We have already covered the 'first-timers'—that is, people who are absolutely terrified of being in a place where they don't know anyone and think they do not belong. This can be handled in a number of ways.

1.  Prepare a standard name tag, either on the computer with a label or by hand. It is important that you make these legible from at least four feet away. No doubt you can imagine the challenge there is when the name tags

are written in type around the size of the printing in this book—you can't read it. As a presenter, I always think what a waste of time and effort it is when organisers provide illegible name tags. From the front of the room you have no chance of reading their names.

Depending on the formality of the sessions, first names may be sufficient. The best computer generated name tags I have seen showed the first name in bold type and the second name considerably smaller:

**ROBYN**
HENDERSON

This might seem like a minor point but think for a moment how many people you know who would benefit by wearing glasses and don't wear them. They spend their lives squinting over menus or say 'I'll have what you're having', rather than put on a pair of glasses. Make it easy to communicate with each other.

2.  Another method I have seen is that when you arrive at the registration desk, you are asked to place one of your business cards in the lucky door prize barrel and use another business card as a name tag, inserting it in a clear plastic name tag holder. This works well as long as the person has a business card. Those that don't may already feel very embarrassed before they enter the room.

    Regarding this plastic name tag holder, the pin-on ones are cheaper, the clip-on ones are a little more expensive. The clip-on ones are well received by women and men alike as they do not damage the fabric they are clipped on to, unlike the pin-on ones. A word of warning also with sticky labels, do a test first to see that they do not mark fabric before you ask people to slap a label on their expensive suit.

    The cards for the lucky door prize allow you to keep the names and addresses of the people attending the function. Some may be guests of members and you will not have their contact details unless you ask for them. The prize does not have to be anything too expensive—for example, flowers, a book, a movie pass, whatever you feel is appropriate for the group.

## Punctuality

It is important that the function starts at the advertised time unless there is something major preventing that. I find guests can become quite hostile if they are not advised of the reason for the delay. Better to start on time and reward those who arrived punctually. At East Coast Business Women's Network we advise 6.30 p.m. for a 7.00 p.m. start. That way, it is clear what time the event will begin.

Finishing time is also important. I strongly believe for mid-week events (dinners, presentations, fashion shows etc.) 10 p.m. is the latest finishing time. Many people have to travel quite a distance home and, if it is a business network, early morning starts are the norm. Again, if you expect something to go later than 10 p.m., advise this on the invitation or at the start of the meeting.

All of these little details help to make it a great function. Believe me, great functions do not just happen, they are planned detail by detail.

## Self-introductions

So you have started on time, introduced yourself and welcomed the group to the event. Depending on the size of the audience, self-introductions are a great way of getting networking happening straight away. At East Coast Business Women's Network, our cut-off point for audiences is 100 people as we like to include self-introductions for everyone in the room.

The skill is in showing people how to introduce themselves in less than 15 seconds, remembering that people switch off after about 15 words. Ask people to give their name and what they do in less than 15 seconds—for example, 'Good evening, I'm Robyn Henderson, Australia's networking specialist and I turn small companies into large companies through networking.'

Without fail, you will have people who will want to waffle on and on and treat this opportunity as a two-minute commercial. What these people don't realise is that the rest of the audience actually switches off from them instantly because they are abusing the privilege. They do themselves more damage than good.

What I have sometimes done, mid-spiel, with these people is interrupt them politely and point out that the chef is waiting to send in our main course and unfortunately we don't have time for everyone to do a commercial, just a brief introduction will have to do tonight. It is interesting to note that these people are often non-members, there for the first time and you never see them again as people avoid them on principle all night.

If all this seems like too much trouble, you really need to ask yourself why you are running this function in the first place. If it is just to make money, forget it. If you want to help to grow people's businesses, this is the way to do it. It is important that people know who everyone in the room is. Why? So they can make contact with them later that evening. An alternative with a large group (more than 100) is to include as part of the program a five minute spot where each table of 10 has their own introductions. This creates extremely loud noise levels but really lifts the energy in the room, at the same time encouraging people to exchange business cards.

What you are basically doing is giving people permission to speak to strangers. Otherwise they will sit there all night, with an ideal prospect across the table from them and never even get to speak to them, as many people's pre-conditioning prevents them from doing so.

So, you have had the self-introductions and everyone knows who everyone is. What you have done is set up the perfect networking environment. It is not up to the organisers to personally introduce A to B. They can now do it themselves.

## Networking tables

A table where people are encouraged to place a small stack of their business cards is a great way for the shyer people to see who is in the room. Remember those first-timers? If they have a great time tonight, they will be back. If not, you have lost them and they will tell others what a lousy time they had. People can mingle around the business card or networking table and feel quite comfortable chatting.

I suspect this fear of talking to people we have not met has something to do with being told as children that we must not talk to strangers. We have to destroy this belief when in the networking environment—talking to strangers is what it is all about.

## Networking breaks

Have you ever been to a function where the organisers kept the schedule so tight that you did not even have time to visit the toilets, let alone network with anyone other than the two people sitting next to you? This is a fatal mistake in function planning. The people are there to network.

If it is evening, they generally want to hear an entertaining speaker with a message. If it is breakfast, they are not looking for entertainment, they got up an hour earlier to be there—they want content and information. At lunches they are really looking for a combination of all of the above. They have to justify why they are at the lunch to their boss or themselves. If they can pick up a few tips, not to mention exchange a few cards, their boss will be satisfied.

It is therefore important to schedule in an official networking break where people are encouraged to move out of their seats—and their comfort zones— exchange cards and network. Prior to the break, tell them what it is all about, put a time limit on it and stand back to avoid the rush. People will go everywhere, you have given them permission to speak to strangers, generate business, exchange cards and meet new people. Great stuff!

## Seating

One of the final points about networking functions is to encourage people from the same company not to sit side by side with each other. If they are really serious about networking, by all means let two or three of them sit at the same table (not side by side). Can you imagine how silly it sounds when eight out of 10 people at a table all stand up and say 'I'm so and so from X company'

... 'me too'. . . 'me too'. I realise it is great to get to see some of your work mates out of work as you get to know them on a different level. However, they should work out their plan before they get to the function and establish whether they are there for business building or to have dinner together.

## Corporate tables

Corporate tables are a great way of gaining recognition for your company, entertaining some of your clients and generating business. Again, seat just a few staff members at the table, introduce your clients to other people they may like to do business with at the function. We will talk more about this in Chapter 14—Revenue enhancement.

Most organisers will let you place a company logo at your table if you have booked and pre-paid for a full table of guests. As an organiser, you are giving your networking function guests an opportunity to be seen, get known, move ahead.

## Ask for help

Don't be afraid to ask for help from volunteers to work on the registration desk, meet and greet or to clean up at the end. Most people are delighted to be asked and if they are not, they will soon tell you. Networking is about sharing. It is a huge task to put together a successful function. Most guests have no idea of the backroom dramas that may be happening.

Total honesty is the best way to handle anything unforeseen. A number of times I have under-catered for functions. This usually happens when fifty people book and pre-pay and 60 people arrive at the door.

Commercially, you do not want to turn people away. However, you realise this blow-out in numbers may cause a challenge in the kitchen. Be honest at the start of the evening. Humorously thank everyone for coming, including the 10 unexpected.

For instance, you can say something along the lines of: 'There may be a minor delay in the meal service, I apologise for this ahead of time. Next month, we would love to receive your prepaid booking prior to the event so as not to inconvenience you again.'

## Catering for vegetarians

Can you imagine how annoying it is to be at a function that you have paid $50 to attend and not be able to eat anything? One of the quickest ways to lose potential members is not to cater for vegetarians. As more and more people choose vegetarianism as a lifestyle, it is important that you have a small box on the registration form to mark if a vegetarian meal will be required. If they don't tick the box, that is their responsibility, not yours.

## Give recognition to the caterers

With the East Coast Business Women's Network in Sydney we are fortunate to have a great working relationship with a number of five star hotels that we have been frequenting for the last few years. Each year we give the waiting staff and the kitchen staff Christmas gifts and a certificate of appreciation for their efforts throughout the year.

We are certainly one of their smaller customers, however the good will that we generate is worth a million dollars. I worked in hospitality for 13 years and was well aware that when you work in the kitchen, generally all you receive by way of feedback is dirty dishes. In our own small way we give recognition to the people who make us look good.

## Wins of the month/week/day

We have already spoken about keeping a success log on a regular basis to record our wins. Giving people an opportunity to share their wins is another great way to increase networking. Slotting a spot on the program, where you briefly give, say, five or six people an opportunity to share their wins is a great lift to the event.

Be patient, you generally have to wait for one person to volunteer to be the first before the others will follow suit. If you have inside information on a win for someone in the room, you may like to be the first to start by nominating that person.

## Numbers

Don't get caught up on numbers by thinking that if it is a small group, it won't work. Numbers are not what networking is about. At a networking function, it is really about creating a really positive energy in the room. One of the ways to do this is to get people talking to each other and sharing ideas. Humour is also a great release for tension and discomfort. There is generally something funny that may have happened that day, share it with the group.The more real you appear in your role as MC, the more the people will respond to you, and the more they will enjoy themselves.

To summarise, plan, plan and plan. Leave nothing to chance. Ask for reliable volunteers who understand what networking is all about. Finally, enjoy yourself!

## 12

# The 'do's and 'don't's of networking

This chapter will summarise a number of points scattered throughout the book, in addition to the many no-nos.

## 'Do's (when attending a networking function)

○ Remember your business cards. Have at least 50 cards on you at any one time. Additional cards may be kept in your car, briefcase, wallet, coat pocket. Most importantly, women often change handbags or switch briefcases as they go from one function to another. The ideal situation is to have cards in every bag.

○ Carry blank cards in case you meet people who do not have business cards with them. You often find that people you have given a blank card to, will approach you again at the function to ask for a few spare cards.

○ Always carry two pens. One for you, one for your new found friend who forgot theirs.

○ Always carry your diary. At networking functions, you are often invited to other functions. You can often miss this opportunity, purely because you cannot give a 'yes' or 'no' answer on the spot.

○ Look out for first-timers—that is, people who look a little uncomfortable and out of place. Befriend these people; every best friend was once a perfect stranger.

○ Book and pre-pay any functions you plan to attend. If you cannot attend on the day, send a replacement. Most organisers are charged for no-shows and most will send you an invoice for your non-attendance.

○ Prepare your 15-second introduction that states clearly who you are, what you do and what you specialise in.

○ Turn off your mobile phone during the function. There is nothing worse than listening to a great speaker be interrupted by a beep of a pager. It is even worse when the person answers the call and starts to have a loud conversation. This is a really quick way to turn the whole group against you.

○ If you are a smoker then check the rules on smoking inside the function. Most functions these days have designated smoke-free zones.

○ Do your homework on the group with whom you are attending. Know something about its history, its mission, how long it has been operating.

○ Decide prior to booking what you want to get out from attending. If you just want a meal then go to a restaurant. Don't waste the time of serious networkers who are looking to grow their businesses.

○ Attend at least two meetings before you officially join any group. Get to know some of the people, let them get to know you. If it is not your perfect fit, move on. There are unlimited numbers of networking groups starting up all the time. Find the one that suits your requirements.

○ The group you do join, attend regularly. The more people see you, build a rapport with you and start to develop trust with you, the more business you will generate.

○ Introduce yourself to strangers—this is totally acceptable in the networking environment.

○ Excuse yourself if you find the people you are speaking to do not interest you or, more importantly, do not appear to be interested in you. Look for a friendly face and introduce yourself to them.

○ Arrive on time. Latecomers arriving with two friends and expecting to sit together can be disappointed when they find only single seats left.

○ Wear your name tag on the right hand side. When you shake hands with someone they will still be able to read your name without obstruction.

○ Make eye contact when you are speaking to people

○ Offer assistance to the host, maybe you could meet and greet visitors, assist with the registration desk, put out brochures. They may decline but they will definitely remember you offered.

○ Read the daily paper or listen to the latest news on the day of the event. Select one or two topics that you will feel confident introducing into the conversation.

○ If you are unsure of the dress code, phone the organiser prior to the event. You may feel quite uncomfortable if you are decidedly over or under dressed.

○ Listen actively—nod, make eye contact, unfold your arms.

○ Move out of your comfort zone.

○ Have fun.

○ Compliment the speaker if you enjoyed their presentation.

○ Follow up if you say you will. Most salespeople miss out on sales because they don't follow up.

○ Attend at least one networking function each week.

○ If possible, give away at least one lead or referral at the function.

○ By the end of the function, if you are thinking it has been a perfect waste of time and you have not generated any business for yourself, find someone you can give some business to. With the law of reciprocity, what you give out is what you get back.

## 'Don't's (when attending a networking function)

○ Unless you are the host, you do not have to speak to everyone in the room when there are more than 20 people attending. Do not 'work' the room. Rather, have a number of quality conversations with the people that cross your path. Leave a positive image with these people and they will spread the word for you.

○ Don't forget your business cards, blank cards, pen and diary.

○ Don't drink excessively—it is not a good look with a room full of strangers. Everything in moderation.

○ Don't leave early unless it is absolutely necessary. Some of the best networking opportunities happen when you arrive early and leave late.

○ Don't monopolise the conversation—networking is about sharing ideas.

○ Don't act like a shark. I am sure you have seen people who 'work the room' by prowling around reading the name tags only, never making eye contact until they find a victim. Then they pounce. Once again, these people are so obvious, most people can see through their behaviour and avoid them at all costs.

○ Don't forget the golden rule—in the networking environment we earn the right to gain business by doing something for someone else first. Don't expect people to place an order with you purely because you have introduced yourself to them. You must earn the right to ask the favour.

○ Don't drop names of people that you don't know and pretend you do. The networking world is very small—you can be caught out very quickly. At the same time, do not bad mouth others as you do not know who these people know.

○ Don't lie about anything. Trust is critical in the networking environment. If you are caught out with a lie, you will do irreparable damage to your reputation.

○ Don't swear or blaspheme as this is inappropriate behaviour.

○ Don't treat the 15-second self-introduction as a two-minute commercial. People will switch off and you will leave a negative impression.

○ Don't jump in when there are pauses in the conversation. Pauses are fine— let the other person jump in first. It may be that they are thinking about their answer.

○ Don't interrupt—only prisoners like to be interrupted in the middle of a sentence.

# 13

## How to market to women via networking groups and special events

This chapter will look at how to market your product to women via networking in a variety of forms. There are subtle differences with marketing to women as against marketing to men. In a nutshell, women want to do business with people they know and trust or with someone who *knows* someone they know and trust.

### Understanding the informal communication channels

Selling in the 1980s was largely about 'what's in it for me?'. There was little regard for customer service, after sales service or service full stop. Many businesses took their customers for granted. As a result, they lost them.

In the 1990s it is a whole new ball game. The Australian market is now wide open for companies and organisations who show their customers and clients how much they care and how important they are to them.

The more trust and rapport a woman has with a supplier (be it a real estate agent, car salesperson, electrician, plumber etc.), the more she will feel inclined to refer business to that person. (Refer to Chapters 2 and 9.) Women need recognition and want to be listened to. Thus, if we want to target women via networking groups and special events, we need to network with them—build relationships and earn the right to ask for the business. Some marketing tools that have successfully worked within these groups include the following.

## Awards

Telstra currently runs the Telstra Business Women's Awards. These awards recognise, encourage and reward Australia's businesswomen. These awards are conducted annually throughout Australia and include the following categories:

○ Business Owner

○ Private Sector—Company employing less than 100 employees

○ Private Sector—Company employing more than 100 employees

○ Public Sector—Government and Agencies

○ State/Territory Telstra Business Woman of the Year

○ Telstra Australian Business Woman of the Year

I attended all the national presentations and they are inspiring events. It was fascinating to see and hear the finalists from each State. I would rate this as a very successful promotion.

## Magazine awards

In July 1994 I was listed in the Top 100 Spirited Women of Australia in *New Woman* magazine. This list was compiled by *New Woman* magazine readers and it was indeed a privilege to be included.

## Club awards

In July 1995, again, I was honoured to receive the 1995 Winning Woman Award from the Zonta Club of Hobart. This is an annual award and the Hobart branch of Zonta is a progressive and forward thinking group.

Most organisations are open and appreciative of sponsorship. With regard to awards, once you have targeted your ideal niche market or group, why not approach them about offering some form of support? This may not take the form of a large award, it could be a small gift for the 'win' of the month, a gift for the guest speaker, or a lucky door prize. This opportunity is not only available for large organisations but also small businesses.

With the East Coast Business Women's Network, we have a wonderful small business sponsor in Bob Forrest from All 4 Flowers in North Sydney. Bob has generously donated beautiful flower arrangements for our guest speakers for a number of years. Naturally, we encourage our members and guests to support his florist. That is as simple as networking is.

## Breakfast clubs

These are another great area for promotion. There are the long-standing groups such as SWAP (Salespeople With A Purpose) as well as the breakfast clubs run by most of the five star hotels. Again, these are a great way to start the day and meet interesting people.

As a professional speaker, it's very exciting and rewarding to present to, say, 200 people at a breakfast—particularly if it is during winter in a cold climate. These people are truly motivated to be there.

Signage can be well placed and well received at these events and sponsored gifts and prizes are always welcomed by the organisers. Obviously, they would not have a situation such as two banks supporting the one event, however there is plenty of room for compatible sponsors.

## Book launches

Book launches are another great way to promote your business. This will, of course, depend on the author, the topic and the expected audience. Maybe the book is about good health or fitness and your business encompasses this area— why not look at a joint production? You can sponsor the invitations, part of the venue and event costs and tie in with the book promotion.

At East Coast Women's Business Network, we encourage our author members to have at least one of their launches at our meetings for a variety of reasons. Mainly, the group is very supportive and will buy lots of books and we are able to give one of our own 'recognition'.

## Mail out sponsorship

Most networking groups have large databases that can be accessed for a fee. Some will just sell you the database. Others will only give you access to their database by including your material in their monthly mail out.

At East Coast Business Women's Network we offer our sponsors an opportunity to access our database of 10 000 businesswomen in the Sydney Metropolitan area for as little as 65 cents per name. The sponsor provides DL folded brochures and we include them with our monthly dinner invitations. In addition, we give the sponsor an opportunity to do a five-minute spot at one of our monthly meetings.

The most successful campaigns have been those where the sponsor attended the meetings for a couple of months, built relationships with the members and guests and, as a result, generated business.

## Seminars

Many of the large conferencing companies are open to negotiation on sponsorship at a variety of their seminars and conferences. Your signage displayed in front of 2000 people at the Convention Centre at Darling Harbour in Sydney for a two-day conference can have quite an impact. Prices vary for this privilege and can be negotiated with the individual companies.

## Sporting events

In the same vein, walk-a-thons, marathons etc. are another area where signage plays an important part. I find t-shirts are great give aways. Most people do some form of exercise and t-shirts are often their preferred form of dress, or maybe they just wear them around the house. Either way, a tasteful t-shirt can be a powerful advertisement for your business.

With all these ideas, don't think your business is too small—it's not. Tapping into networking opportunities will very quickly grow your business into a large concern.

The benefits of using these networking events as a marketing tool include:

O   the ability to identify specific target markets;

O   *an opportunity for* you to cross network groups;

O   an opportunity to be seen to support women in business;

O   the chance to reduce your advertising costs;

O   an opportunity to increase current customer retention; and

O   the chance to turn prospects into customers.

## Hot tips

If you do decide to market to women via the networking groups and associations:

O   *Do your homework.* Research a variety of prospective groups. Attend these groups at least twice before deciding which is the best one for you.

O   *Keep attending before, during and after your sponsorship.* Ideally, you will have a pool of people you can choose from to represent your company. At least one of these people should always be in attendance.

O   *Always negotiate win–win deals.* You sell your product and you assist the network to grow.

O   *Aim for publicity mileage for you and the group.*

O   *Invite clients to your sponsored events.*

O   *Include tracking systems in your promotion to be able to quantify your results.*

O   *Respect these networks and their influence.*

○  *Develop your own databases from supporting these groups.*

Today's networking groups are:

○  diverse;

○  varying in size, profile and missions;

○  growing rapidly; and

○  the perfect vehicle for targeting the corporate women.

## 14

# *Revenue enhancement*

## Making money for your clients

This chapter will look at ways of making money for your clients. I can already hear some of the readers saying, 'You're kidding, I am flat out making money for myself, why would I make money for my client?' Having read this far, you would realise by now that networking is always working in a win–win relationship—that is, earning the right to do business.

Chapters 1 and 2 laid the foundations for understanding how networking turns prospects into advocates, where they become our unpaid salespeople. They refer business to us and we reciprocate. Again, we need systems in place to assist with this process. Otherwise we won't think about doing it until our workload is low.

Imagine a small company of approximately 10 employees selling a consumable product to retailers. The company includes four salespeople, two managers, one administration person and three warehouse staff. The company is growing steadily and has a reasonable customer base. Like most businesses, it doesn't have a lot of clients (customers who buy regularly) and even fewer advocates. It does have a lot of customers though, and the managers know that if they can just get these customers to buy more often and select more from their product range, their business will grow.

Maybe this scenario resembles your own situation. Imagine the management bringing in a new system where they encourage the salespeople and the management to refer one piece of business to someone every day. Perhaps it will be a customer, perhaps someone that they have met out networking—anyone will be suitable.

Now we have six referrals per day going out of that company, five days per week, 52 weeks of that year—this means 1560 referrals per year. Wow, now that's impressive! What the company has done is to change their mindset about how they will grow their business. From now on they will help their customers to grow their businesses. Maybe some of those referrals are to send more people to those retail outlets to, naturally, buy their products. Maybe they have nothing to do with their business at all. Perhaps they just grow other peoples businesses and, at the same time, sit back and watch their own grow.

This scenario may seem totally impractical and perhaps even a little ridiculous to some readers. If that is the case, please skip this chapter. However, if you want to become a really successful networker keep reading.

You may be running a one-person business—flat out all day every day, working very long hours. You really have to force yourself to attend a net-working function each week. And here I am suggesting that you take precious time out to grow other people's businesses. Trust me—try giving a referral away every day for the next 21 days and just see what happens.

What I will suggest to you is that you start asking people that you come in contact with in your line of work—other customers, suppliers, friends, associates—two questions:

*If I met your ideal customer, what would they be like?*
*What would their business look like?*

Once you have asked these questions, listen to the response and take notes on their business card. My own experience with this has been that I did not know these people did half the things that they do. I could instantly give them a referral and, actually, I could have given them that referral months ago had I known exactly who they were looking for. Now that I do know who they are looking for I file that information away, either in my customer card or client file, and I make a mental note to look out for their ideal customer. Think for a moment how many clients you come into contact with each day. You could ask this question many times over and start to grow your own information file of potential referrals.

The next step is to slot in five minutes per day of your networking time, and classify these five minutes as 'referral time'. This is the time each day when, if you have not had the opportunity to give away a referral, do so now. We are really aiming to discipline ourselves into developing this habit.

As good networkers, we should stop focussing on what we want and look at who we can help. We are really earning the right to ask a favour here—big time. As a busy professional speaker I am often invited to speak at conferences and sometimes I am already booked for another presentation in another city, so I can't do it. Rather than let my client down, I ask if they would like me to suggest another speaker for the session. Ninety nine per cent of the time they are grateful for my offer. So I generally discuss the brief with them, get an idea of their budget and fax or phone a couple of speakers. Explaining the situation, I ask them to contact the client directly, either by phone or fax, sending a recent profile and confirming their availability and fee for the session. It is then up to the client to make their selection. One successful speaker in this scenario rang me back, thanking me for the lead and asking how much I wanted as a spotter's fee. They were quite surprised when I said I did not want any part of a fee. My sole request was that they would do a first class presentation, make the client look good and make sure the audience had fun and learned something at the same time.

My logic was, if this speaker made the client look good, I looked good and the client was satisfied. Hopefully, when an opportunity arises again when he needs a speaker and doesn't know where to find one for a certain topic, he will phone me, I will be able to refer work to someone else, they will do a great job, the client will look good and the networking chain keeps growing and growing.

## Turning every customer into an advocate overnight

I have observed that when people attract new customers (particularly if large orders are generated) they generally talk about their new customers with their peer group. The obvious question asked from the peer group is: 'How did you get that customer?'

'Oh, my plumber referred them to me.'

'Your plumber, you are kidding! Your plumber referred you to this customer who just placed a $10 000 order with you?'

'That's right, their company believes in networking, in helping their customers grow their business. Funny thing is we have been thinking about putting in a new bathroom in our home so we've asked the plumber to quote for the job. His quote was higher than the others, but he is extremely reliable and has certainly earned the right to get repeat business from me, would you agree?'

'What is the name and phone number of this plumber? I want to meet this guy.'

You will be overwhelmed with the response you receive when you start to give away referrals regularly. People are blown away by your generosity. The law of reciprocity steps in and before you know it they are talking about you, saying how impressed they are with your behaviour, and your phone starts ringing.

For the doubting Thomases who may be reading this, I have built my business on the networking principle of earning the right to do business. At the time of writing, I have been running a small business for four years. In that time I have fast tracked my professional speaking career and for the last three years have done in excess of 230 speaking engagements each year.

Speaking engagements are really no different to other businesses, you do one engagement, you have a customer. If they invite you back, you have a client. If you don't lose that customer through inferior service, that person will use your services again and again and, ultimately, become your advocate. If you can refer business to that client, they will stand out from your competitors—it is as simple as that. So how can you start referring business to your customers?

○ Find out who your clients' potential customers are. Ask the two questions mentioned on page 90 and listen to the answers.

○ Show as much interest in their business as you do in your own.

○ Promise good, deliver great. Don't promise them you will have a lead for them if you are not completely confident you can do it. Exceed their expectations each time you make contact with them.

○ Prepare a sheet to include in your diary:

| Date | Contact person | Referred to: | Method: | Follow up |
|------|----------------|--------------|---------|-----------|
| Today | John Smith (builder) | Jack Jones (real estate agent/ developer) | by fax | 4 weeks (date) |

This instantly shows that you have referred John Smith, your reliable builder, to Jack Jones (a real estate agent who told you he was looking for a builder to take on a small development project). You sent the information by fax and you will follow up four weeks from today and see what has developed. You have also faxed John Smith so he will be expecting the contact from Jack.

Always remember the KISS system—Keep it Simple Stupid. It is important to get back to both sides of the referral so that you can monitor it. If you find that either party has not delivered the goods and they do not have a good explanation for this, don't refer anymore business to that person. Unfortunately, we learn the hard way that some people are less reliable than others.

In 1995, I started running revenue enhancement networking breakfasts with some of my real estate and insurance clients. Admittedly, they were a little reluctant at first, but they soon saw how beneficial they were in giving recognition to their client base. I suggested to these people that they invite clients (past and present) to the breakfast. If they wanted 50 people, they should invite 75 as there would be a number of no-shows. The clients paid a small fee to come to the breakfast and this virtually covered the cost of the food and my fee. The format was similar to the function I outlined in Chapter 6. We gave people name tags and had the self-introductions before encouraging the exchange of business cards.

After a presentation outlining how they could support and grow their local community through networking effectively, we did an 'ask for help'. Here, we encouraged each person briefly to ask for help from the group. Although the first couple of 'asks' were very shy, we soon had people describing their businesses and asking if anyone knew anyone who wanted their product or service. Without fail, with every request, at least one person in the room said, 'Yes, I know someone, who needs … See me when we finish.' The breakfasts were a huge success and it was great to see so many people mingling after the event, exchanging more cards and business tips. The real estate and insurance clients looked great and their clients were still talking about it months later. Once you start to make money for your client, your own business will grow beyond your expectations.

Try the 'give away a referral a day' for the next 21 days and plot your results. You may be pleasantly surprised with both the response and the results.

This chapter covered an area that many people are reluctant to try. I would encourage you to develop this daily referral habit. It alone has been responsible for a huge growth in my business as well as my clients'. Combined with the other ideas in the book, it will really set you apart from the run-of-the-mill networker.

## KEY POINT
*Exceed people's expectations constantly and watch your business prosper.*

# Networking ethics

In this chapter we need to refer to the Bible:

*Do unto others as you would have them do unto you.*

That explains networking ethics in a nutshell.

---

List the names of three people in your life who have done the wrong thing by you in business and how they did this.

1. _____

2. _____

3. _____

How do you feel now about doing business with     Yes          No
these people? Do you trust them?
(circle your response)

Would you refer business to them?                 Yes          No

---

## Integrity or nothing

In today's world, competition is fierce enough without people thinking less of us because of our poor behaviour. The 1990s is the decade of integrity and for those of us who have always lived and worked with integrity, our time has come at last.

Many high flyers and entrepreneurs in the 1980s got to the top of the ladder by climbing over people and working on a win–lose basis. Many of these people and their businesses are no longer operating. Now in the 1990s, the consumer is more astute, more demanding and more aware. They insist on doing business with people they know and trust. Trust is the glue that keeps the relationship going. When we promise good and delivery lousy, we break this trust.

There are a limited number of businesses that have no competitors. Those that do, have this monopoly for a very short time. It is critical in the networking world that we always deal with integrity and honesty. The truth, no matter how bad it is, cannot hurt you. Lies, on the other hand, can destroy you and your reputation.

Recently, I gave a networking presentation to a small group of business operators. During question time I was asked about my photograph business cards, where I bought them and how much they were. At the time, I related the networking story of how I came to have the business cards sponsored by a company who specialised in business cards. One of their managers had seen an article on business cards that I had written, contacted me to ask if he could reproduce the article and offered to supply my cards for me. I was appreciative of the offer and pointed out that I currently use around 1000 business cards each month and if he was happy to supply that many, I would be grateful.

The printer includes his phone number in small type on the back of my business card, to make it easy for people to contact him if they want a similar card. As I had been asked this many times, I was happy to share the information and the cost.

Two days later, I was working interstate and had a call from my office advising me that the printer had rung in a most concerned state. He had had a call from one of the audience demanding that he give them the same deal he had struck with me—1000 free cards per month. The printer was confused and concerned as he had not had a call like this before and wanted to know:

○  what he should do about it; and

○  had I altered the 'rules' without letting him know?

I was horrified with this person for jeopardising my sponsorship with this printer. I phoned the person and expressed my disappointment with them. Pointing out that there were many printers available—no doubt they had already established a relationship with a printer—why not approach them and ask if they could negotiate a win–win deal. This to me was not ethical behaviour and is a perfect example of networking without ethics.

On a much smaller scale, I recently spent time bartering my services with someone who wanted to network with lawyers and insurance managers. I had a number of these people in my network and agreed to write a letter to 10 of them advising that this person would be contacting them within seven days. I asked if, as a favour to me, they could spare five minutes on the phone giving her assistance with her project.

Three weeks later, I have received faxes and phone calls from seven of the group of 10 just to let me know they are still waiting for the phone call from my 'friend'. They are all great networkers and this is how it happens. Don't ask for referrals if you are not going to use them immediately. Let the referee know this is a future project. Don't waste people's time. Value their time as much as you value your own.

I am unsure if integrity is a learned skill or something we develop in our childhood as a belief system. One thing is certain though, poor ethics in the networking environment will destroy you. Loyalty is paramount. You don't know who knows who or what their remote connection is. Be assured however, bad news travels fast. In the networking world, ranks will close around you to exclude you and protect their network from you.

## KEY POINT
*Always work with integrity—it is the only way to survive and grow.*

# 16

## Ask for what you want

This chapter will look at combining what we want in our life with networking. If we learn to ask for what we want, we will get it. How many times have you heard your partner, friend, boss, child make the comment: 'If you don't tell me what you want, I can't give it to you'? This is critical in the networking environment if we are to achieve our goals and make networking really work for us.

### Identifying your current goals

I have lost count of the number of calls I have from people saying things like:

1. I am really struggling with my business, can you refer someone to me?

2. I am looking for work, do you know anyone who would give me a job?

3. I need more customers, help me.

4. I hate my job, do you know any others that are available?

My response to all of these is that you must be clearer with your request or you will never get what you want.

You don't want just any job, customer or lead, you want a specific one. The more specific you are with your needs, the more chance you have of getting exactly what you want. Near enough is not good enough.

Rephrased, the above examples can become:

1. I am trying to grow my business and am looking specifically for small businesses with around a $100 000 plus turnover who may be looking for someone to do their books.

2. I am currently unemployed and have had 10 years' experience in the hospitality industry. I believe tourism is still a growth area, but am prepared to start at the bottom and work my way up. Do you know anyone who could use my services?

3. I am experiencing a rocky road with my retail business and I would appreciate connecting with any people who may be interested in some great bargains in smart casual and resort wear. Do you know anyone who may be interested in my offer of two garments for the price of one?

4. I have been in the retail area for 15 years and I have grown stale in my present position. Do you know anyone who may be able to utilise my great sales ability, enthusiasm and eye for detail? My target is a new job by November 1.

The clearer you are, the more you can be helped.

---

In fewer than 10 words how would you describe your life at present?

_____

_____

In fewer than 10 words describe how you would like your life to be:

1. 12 months from now. _____

2. 5 years from now. _____

What specifically do you need to take you from your present situation to:

1. your one-year vision? _____

2. your five-year vision? _____

To achieve your one or five-year vision Do you     Yes          No
need to reskill? (circle your response)

continued …

| If yes, do you have all the relevant information on courses available? | Yes | No |
|---|---|---|

If not, who do you have to contact for this information? _____
When can you make that contact? _____

| Would it be wise to expand your networks to assist with actualising this vision? | Yes | No |
|---|---|---|

If yes, which network should you connect with? _____

| Is there someone in your current network who could help you if they knew your plans? | Yes | No |
|---|---|---|

If yes, identify that person and then decide when you could make contact with them. _____

What budget do you need to achieve your visions? _____

List ways you may be able to finance this budget.

The whole reason for writing down our thoughts here is that the act of writing something down can trigger a response in our subconscious. The more we think about something, the more chance we have of making it happen.

## How can networking help you achieve these goals?

In our preparation in attending networking functions, we need to be really clear on:

○ why we are going; and

○ what we hope to achieve by attending the event.

If we are clear on what we want and can specifically detail this, we can ask for help. From personal experience, I know that asking for help was one of the hardest things I had to learn to do. I would reinvent the wheel rather than ask someone to show me how something was done.

I wrote and self-published my two previous books *Networking For $uccess* and *Are You the VIP in your Life?* with next to no computer or publishing skills. This year I completed a short computer course and my life became immeasurably easier.

I have often found in women a reluctance to ask for help. Many of us have such an independent streak and resist anyone helping us. Again, networking is really about feeling okay about asking for help. If I ask you for something and you can't help me, you will introduce me to someone who can.

Win–win–win, we are all happy. Be warned though! Sometimes we resent help. Often when I have been asked for advice or help, I will ask of the person:

○ How badly do you want this?

○ What are you prepared to do or to do without to make it happen?

○ What is the best possible outcome if this does happen?

○ What is the worst possible outcome if this happens?

○ Can you cope with the worst possible scenario?

This normally sorts out 'wants' versus 'needs' and there is generally quite a gap between the two.

The next question then follows:

○ What is the first step you have to take to get the ball rolling to make your vision happen?

An example of the above scenario may be someone unhappy in their job and looking for a career move. You might ask them to answer the questions provided above—the key question being: What are they prepared to do or to do without to make it happen? For example:

○ Would they move to another State for the right position?

○ Would they take a drop in salary to get a foot in with X Company?

○ Have they applied for many jobs as yet?

○ Have they selected a company they would like to work for?

○ If so, how much research have they done on this company?

○ What is their alternative plan if they do not get into this company?

Be warned—when you ask a successful networker for help, they may grill you as I have done. Basically they will want to know how badly you want it. If you don't want it badly enough, there will be someone else behind you who does, and they will get it.

In summary, be clear on what you want, ask for it and then be prepared to do whatever it takes to get it.

*17*

# *Checklist for effective networkers*

This chapter will move you into the networking world quickly and safely by having you define what your present and future networking needs are.

**Monthly action plan**

This week I need to purchase (tick as required):

Stationery

Business Cards ☐

Business Card Holder ☐

(office ) ☐

(functions) ☐

Thank You Cards ☐

Birthday Cards ☐

*continued ...*

Sympathy Cards ☐

Everyday Cards ☐

With Compliments Slips ☐

Letterhead ☐

Envelopes ☐

Blank Cards ☐

Diary ☐

*Magazine subscriptions*

Which industry magazines should I be reading? _____

Networking functions _____

What groups should I contact to ask to be put on the mailing list? _____

What groups should I ask to be removed from their mailing list? _____

Which of my memberships are due for renewal? _____

What networking groups will I go to this month? (recommended one per week)

|  | Name | Date | Time |
|---|---|---|---|
| 1. |  |  |  |
| 2. |  |  |  |
| 3. |  |  |  |
| 4. |  |  |  |

Have I registered and prepaid for these functions?     Yes     No

Have I booked to attend any functions and now am     Yes     No
not available? If unavailable, who could I give this
invitation to? _____

Is there anyone I can invite to the functions I am
attending? _____

Will I seek out sponsorship opportunities with a     Yes     No
networking group this month?

**Yearly action plan**

What companies would I like to do business with in the next year?

1.

2.

3.

What past customers would I like to do business with this year?

What customers can I aim to turn into clients this year?

What clients can I aim to turn into advocates this year?

What can I do to get the ball rolling with the above clients?

Does my stationery need a revamp?        Yes        No

What image do I want to project with my company?

Are there any competitors that I could approach regarding some joint ventures next year?

Do I need to reskill at all this year?        Yes        No

If yes, which skills need my attention?

Am I scheduling weekly 15-minute meetings with my staff to update them on the progress of the company?

Do all my staff have business cards?        Yes        No

Are they using them?        Yes        No

How long since my staff reordered business cards?

What is my main goal or target for the coming year?

How can networking help me achieve this goal?

The aim of this chapter was to have you think about your current and future networking needs. You may choose to take this personal stocktake more often. Being organised is critical to enable you to maximise your networking time.

## 18

# *Where will I go to network?*

There is an unlimited number of global networking groups. Some are run more formally than others. I recommend that you do not join any of the networks until you have attended at least two functions: first, to make sure the group is definitely what you are looking for; and second, to make sure that the group will consistently be able to meet your needs.

You will be better off financially if you pay the additional cost of attending as a non-member for individual meetings than if you pay a full year's membership and then only attend a few times in that period.

## Some recommended networks

### East Coast Business Women's Network
*New South Wales*
PO Box 195
Coogee NSW 2034
Phone (02) 9369 1025  Fax (02) 9369 1053

*Queensland*
PO Box 592
Mermaid Beach Qld 4218
Phone (07) 5592 2915  Fax (07) 5526 7917

*Victoria*
PO Box 235
East Bentleigh Vic 3165
Phone (03) 9209 1640   Fax (03) 9364 8718

### Business and Professional Women (National group)
GPO Box 2544
Sydney NSW 2001
Phone (02) 9413 4244   Fax (02) 9413 4263

### Chief Executive Women Inc.
Phone (02) 9953 2900   Fax (02) 9953 1741

### Dynamis Club
46A Kulgoa Road
Pymble NSW 2073
Phone (02) 9440 8226   Fax (02) 944 1631

### Enterprising Women
PO Box 740
Gymea NSW 2227
Phone (02) 9545 4718   Fax (02) 9521 6529

### National Enterprising Women in Business (NEWIB)
Level 12
83 Clarence Street
Sydney NSW 2000
Phone (02) 9350 8100   Fax (02) 9350 8199

### Rural Women's Network (NSW)
c/- NSW Agriculture
Locked Bag 21
Orange NSW 2800
Phone (063) 91 3611    Fax (063) 91 6350

### Zonta International (National Group)
PO Box A2472
Sydney South NSW 2000
Phone (02) 9267 3855   Fax (02) 9264 3670

Although the groups listed above are predominantly women's groups, this is not to say that there are no male networking groups available. Consult your yellow pages telephone book and local papers for lists of networking groups available in your area. If you can't find one in your area, why not start one yourself?

## Highly recommended

○ Regional Business Enterprise Centres

○ State and regional chambers of commerce

○ Toastmasters International

○ National Speakers Association of Australia

## The future of networking

This book is dedicated to my nieces Kate and Greer—aged 11 and 1 respectively. What does networking hold for their future? The world is changing at such a rapid rate, communication systems are being upgraded constantly. Networking is becoming a way of life, an actual lifestyle. It is not something that you do during business hours, but rather something that is done twenty-four hours a day. Networking groups will continue to flourish. Those that constantly keep their members involved and informed of business opportunities and those that can adapt to change the fastest will survive. Those that retain old ideas and formats will fall by the wayside.

As advanced as technology is becoming, I doubt that anything will ever replace the humble business card. It may have bells, whistles and sound included in it and it may ultimately be made from material other than carboard. Despite any changes that may occur to the business card as we know it today, it will always be your introduction to those wonderful future members of your personal network.

Let's wave the magic wand for the final time today and envisage a world where networking is the *only* way that business is done globally. There is no competition, only cooperation. There is no unemployment, job sharing is an accepted form of employment. Cross networking with clients and customers is commonplace.

As one business grows and prospers it triggers a chain of reaction with all the other businesses it is associated with. Down the line another business prospers, and another, and another... until every business is operating to its absolute capacity.

Employees and employeers alike are happy and healthy, daily receiving recognition for jobs well done. Prosperity is everywhere as all contracts are

*Where will I go to network?*

negotiated with a win-win focus. There are no losers or winners.

This is the global network of the future. How long before this becomes a reality? That's really up to us. If everyone who reads this book shares it with another and another and another, before long this global network will be our reality.

Happy networking.

# references

Covey, S. R. (1990), *The Seven Habits of Highly Effective People*, Information Australia, Melbourne.

Kennedy, I. and Cowtenay, B. (1995), *The Power of One on One*, Margaret Gee Publishing, Sydney.

Merrill, Roger, Merril, Rebecca and Covey, S. R. (1994), *First Things First*, Simon and Schuster, New York.

# *i* n d e x

# Australian Institute of Management

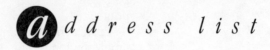

# address list

If you would like more information on your local AIM bookshop, please contact your State branch at the following addresses.

**NEW SOUTH WALES**

Mailing address
PO Box 328
North Sydney NSW 2059

Locations
215 Pacific Highway
North Sydney NSW 2059
(Opp. Motor Registry)
Ph:  02 9956 3999
Fax: 02 9956 5636

80 George Street
Cnr Horwood Place
Paramatta NSW 2150
Ph:  02 9893 8477
Fax: 02 9893 7650

Web home page
http://www.ozemail.com.au/~a
imbooks
EMAIL
aimbooks@ozemail.com.au

**VICTORIA**

Mailing address
PO Box 112
St Kilda Victoria 3182

Locations
90 Swan Street
Richmond Victoria 3121
Ph:  03 9534 8181
Fax: 03 9428 5781

707 Mount Alexander Road
Moone Ponds Victoria 3039
Ph:  03 9326 1267
Fax: 03 9326 1268

**QUEENSLAND AND
NORTHERN TERRITORY**

Mailing address
PO Box 200
Spring Hill Queensland 4000

Location
Cnr Boundary and Rosa Streets
Spring Hill Queensland 4000
Ph:  07 3832 1412
Fax: 07 3932 2497
Free Call: 1 800 172 085

**SOUTH AUSTRALIA**

Management House
224 Hindley Steet
Adelaide South Australia 5000
Ph:  08 212 3166
Fax: 08 231 2414

**WESTERN AUSTRALIA**

Mailing address
PO Box 195
Wembley WA 6014

Location
76 Birkdale Street
Floreat Western Australia 6014

Ph:  09 387 7788
Fax: 09 383 7056

**TASMANIA**

Mailing address
GPO Box 1069
Hobart Tasmania 7001

Location
1st Floor
130 Collins Street
Hobart Tasmania 7000
Ph:  002 24 2559
Fax: 002 24 2549